On Signs

And Other Essays

By

St. Ignatius Brianchaninov

"I write it myself, edit it myself, censor it myself, publish it myself, distribute it myself, and spend time in prison for it myself."
– **Vladimir Konstantinovich Bukovsky**

Samizdat Press
First Edition – 7528 AM
All Products of Samizdat Press Sold at Manufacturing Cost

Table of Contents

Table of Contents 1
On Signs and Miracles 3
On the Deadening of the Human Spirit..31
On Vigilance 38
On Reading The Gospels 41
On Reading the Holy Fathers...45
The Activity of Prayer Is the Highest Activity of the Human Mind 48
Learn to Pray to God in the Right Way 50
Do Not Seek Enjoyment in Prayer...54
On Spiritual Deception 59

St. Ignatius Brianchaninov

On Signs and Miracles

Introduction

The Holy Gospel tells us that the Pharisees, not satisfied with the miracles performed by our Lord, demanded from Him a particular miracle, *a sign from heaven* (Mark 8:1). A demand for such a sign, consistent with a strange understanding of miracles and signs, was repeated more than once, as the Lord testified: *Why doth this generation seek after a sign* (Mark 8:12)? The Sadducees took part in the Pharisees' demand, though their belief was different from that of the Pharisees. The desire for a sign from heaven was sometimes expressed by the people too; and this after the miraculous multiplying of the five loaves and the feeding of the multitude, when there were five thousand men present, and women and children. Yet the eyewitnesses of this miracle, the participants of this meal, said to the Lord: *What sign shewest Thou then, that we may see, and believe Thee?... Our fathers did eat manna in the desert; as it is written, He gave them bread from Heaven to eat* (John 6:30 31).

The miraculous multiplication of the loaves in the hands of the Saviour seemed insufficient to them. This was done quietly, with the holy humility in which all of the God man's actions were imbued, but the people needed a spectacle, they needed something which produced an effect. They needed the skies to be covered by dense clouds, for the thunder to roll and the lightning to dazzle, and the loaves to fall from heaven.

The demand for a miracle from the Lord by the chief priests and the elders was characterised by the same spirit, for when the Lord freely willed to be lifted upon the Cross, *the chief priests mocking,* the Gospel tells us, *with the scribes and elders, said He saved others; Himself He cannot save. If He be the King of Israel; let Him now come down from the Cross, and we will believe Him (Matt. 27:41, 42).* They accepted the miracles performed by the Lord as miracles and yet they scorned them and jeeringly denied the miracles bestowed by the Divine philanthropy of God, and demanded a miracle of their own invention and discretion, a miracle which, if it were to occur, would have destroyed the purpose of the coming to earth of the God man, and there would have been no salvation for mankind.

Herod was also among those who wanted to see a miracle from the Lord to amuse their curiosity, their heedless imprudence. Herod wanted a sign as a pleasant diversion, and not receiving what he desired, he rained abuse on the Lord, thus giving himself a moment of distraction.

What did it signify, this common demand for a miracle from the Lord, a demand expressed by people of such different directions, combined with a disdain for the [truly] amazing miracles of our Lord? Such a demand was an expression of human sophistry towards miracles. What is a carnal mind? It is a way of thinking about God and all that is spiritual, based on man's fallen condition, and not on the Word of God. The nature of defiance and hostility towards God with which this carnal mindedness is filled shows itself with particular clarity in the demand for miracles from the Lord according to an understanding of false wisdom, inattention to the miracles, and a denial and rejection of the miracles accomplished by Christ through His ineffable goodness. He performed them, being *the power of God, and the wisdom of God* (I Cor. 1:24).

Part I

It was a serious sin to demand a miracle from the Lord, a demand inspired by carnal mindedness. Upon hearing this insolent and blasphemous demand, our Lord sighed deeply in His spirit and saith, *Why doth this generation seek after a sign? Verily I say unto you, there shall no sign be given unto this generation. And He left them, and entering into the ship again departed...* (Mark 8:12,13).

There is joy in heaven over one repenting sinner, and, on the contrary, there is sorrow among the heavenly dwellers over a man falling into sin and his denial of repentance (Luke 15:10). In his blessed contemplation of the infinite goodness of God towards mankind, in his contemplation of the good will of God that all men should be saved, the great Saint Macarius deigned to say that the All holy, dispassionate God experiences divine sorrow at the destruction of man. This sorrow which is beyond our understanding, is not alien to the Spirit of God, and the Spirit of God dwelling in us, *Itself maketh intercession for us with groanings which cannot be uttered* (Rom. 8:26). Such sorrow arose in the Son of God by the demand for a miracle, a demand both prideful and unreasonable. He sighed in His Spirit and said, *Why doth this generation seek after a sign* (Mark 8:12)? The question was our Lord's reply to the demand, hostile to God, for a sign. What deep sorrow can be heard, a sorrow of God, in this answer! In it we seem to hear an expression of perplexity created by the folly and impertinence of this demand. We hear the loss of hope for the salvation of those who made the request, which was contrary to the Spirit of the One bestowing salvation.

The Lord departs from those who are bound by human sophistry, stubbornly dwelling in it, without the desire to be healed. He leaves them to themselves, leaves them to their choice of destruction, to which they consciously adhere. *And He left them* (Mark 8:13).

It is natural for the dead not to feel their state, and the carnal understanding does not sense spiritual death. Because of its inability to understand its own ruin, there is no realisation of the need for life, and on the basis of a false view of life, the carnal mind has denied and is denying true life God.

Can a sign from heaven have special authority? Those who demanded such a sign, of course, demanded it because they attributed such authority to it. Can we conclude that a sign from heaven is always a sign from God? The Holy Scripture tells us otherwise. The very expression, 'a sign from heaven', is imprecise: for people living back then and now. Those not acquainted with the sciences understand "heaven" to be that which happens in the realm of the air and sky. The sun, moon, and stars are declared to be in heaven in that they float in space, and rain, thunder and lightning are called manifestations from heaven although, since they occur in the air, it is more proper to associate them with the earth. The Holy Scripture tells us that by the action of the devil, fire from heaven fell and burnt up the sheep and the servants of Job (Job 1:16). Clearly this fire formed in the air just like lightning. Simon the Magician astounded spiritually blind people with miracles, and the power of satan was mistaken as the great power of God (Acts 8:10). Simon particularly astounded the idol worshipping Romans when, at a large gathering, he declared himself a god and his intention to rise in the air, then suddenly started to rise. This is written about by Simeon Metaphrastes, who took the above description from the earliest Christian writers.

It is a terrible misfortune the lack of true knowledge of God in man when one takes the works of the devil for the works of God. Before the Second Coming of Christ, when Christianity, spiritual knowledge, and discernment will become scarce to an extreme, then *there shall arise false Christ's, and false prophets, and shall shew great signs and wonders; insomuch that if it were possible, they shall deceive the very elect* (Matt. 24:24). The antichrist himself will generously lavish miracles upon men, astounding and satisfying the ignorant and carnal minded. He will give them the signs from heaven for which they seek and thirst. *Whose coming,* says the Apostle Paul, *is after the working of satan with all power and signs and lying wonders, and with all deceivableness of unrighteousness in them that perish; because they received not the love of the truth, that they may be saved* (II Thess. 2:19 10). The ignorant and carnal minded, seeing these miracles, will not stop to reason, and because of the affinity of their spirit for the spirit of the miracles, in their blindness will immediately accept the activity of satan as the greatest manifestation of the power of God. The antichrist will be accepted very hastily, without thought. People will not realise that his miracles do not have any blessed, reasonable goal, no definite meaning, that they are alien to truth, play acting deprived of meaning, filled with lies, that they are monstrous, malicious, and meaningless, straining to astonish, deceive and entice by the enchantment of a lavish, empty, silly effect.

It is not strange that the miracles of the antichrist will be accepted without question and with delight by apostates from Christianity—enemies of the truth, and of God. They prepared themselves for an open, active acceptance of the messenger and the instrument of satan, of his teachings and all his actions, having entered into spiritual contact with him at the right moment. It is worthy of thoughtful attention and sorrow to note that the miracles and acts of the antichrist will create difficulty even for the chosen of God. The reason for the strong influence of the antichrist on men will be centred in his hellish corruption and hypocrisy, an artful covering up of the most horrendous evil, in its unrestrained and shameless insolence, in the prolific cooperation of the fallen spirits, and finally in the ability to create miracles that will be false, but astonishing. The human mind is unable to imagine such an evil man, which the antichrist will be. It is not possible for a human heart, even a sinful one, to believe that evil could reach such a level, as it will with the antichrist. He will boast loudly about himself, as his forerunners and his prototypes did, he will call himself a preacher and restorer of the true knowledge of God. The non-discerning Christians will see in him a representative and a supporter of true religion and will thus join him. He will proclaim and call himself the promised Messiah, and the children of carnal wisdom will rush to meet him, proclaim his glory, power, and genius,—will proclaim him a god, become his supporters.

The antichrist will show himself to be meek, merciful, filled with love, filled with all virtue. Those who will acclaim him as such, and will submit to him as the highest good, are they who accept the truth of fallen mankind and will not deny it for the truth of the Gospel.

The antichrist will offer to mankind the most exalted earthly organisation of well being and prosperity. He will offer honour, riches, luxury, enjoyment, physical comfort, and delight. Seekers of earthly things will accept the antichrist and will call him their master. The antichrist will reveal before mankind by means of cunning artifice, as in a theatre, a show of astonishing miracles, unexplainable by contemporary science. He will instil fear by the storm and wonderment of his miracles, and will satisfy the [worldly wise], he will satisfy the superstitious, and he will confound human learning. All men, led by the light of fallen nature, alienated from the guidance of God's Light, will be enticed into submission to the seducer (Rev. 13:8).

The signs of the antichrist will be primarily in the air for it is in this realm that satan mainly rules (Eph. 2:2; 6:12). The signs will act upon the sense of sight, charming and deceiving it. Saint John the Theologian, contemplating events in the world before the end, says in the book of Revelation that the antichrist will perform great deeds *so that he maketh fire come down from heaven on the earth in the sight of men* (Rev. 13:13). The Holy Scriptures point to this phenomenon as the highest of the signs of the antichrist, and the place for this sign is in the aerial realm it will be a magnificent and awesome spectacle. The signs of the antichrist will complement the actions of his cunning conduct; they will seduce the majority of men to follow him. The opponents of the antichrist will be considered as rebels, enemies of the common good and order, and will be subject to covert and open persecution, to torture and execution.

The false spirits, sent throughout the world, will incite in men a generally high opinion of the antichrist, universal ecstasy, irresistible attraction to him. The Holy Scriptures have depicted in numerous ways the forcefulness of the last persecution of Christians and the cruelty of this persecution. A decisive and definite characteristic serves as the name given by the Scriptures to this frightening person he is called the *beast* (Rev. 13:1), just as the fallen archangel is called *a dragon* (Gen. 3:1; Rev. 12:3). These names correctly depict both enemies of God. One acts secretly, the other more openly, but the beast, who is similar to all beasts, unites in himself a wide variety of cruelty, *and the beast which I saw was like unto a leopard, and his feet were as the feet of a bear, and his mouth as the mouth of a lion* (Rev. 13:2), *the dragon gave him his power, and his seat, and great authority* (Rev. 13:2).

A frightening trial will descend upon the holy saints of God: cunning, hypocrisy, and the awesomeness of the persecutor will increase in order to deceive and seduce them. Refined, inventive, concealed by cunning, the persecutions, constraints, and unlimited power of the tormentor will place them in a most difficult situation. Their small number will seem insignificant before mankind, and their opinion will be viewed as weak and feeble; they will endure general disdain, hatred, slander, and oppression. Violent death will be their lot. Only with the special help of Divine Grace and under its guidance, will the elect of God be able to stand against the enemy of God, to confess the Lord Jesus before him and before men.

The reason for discussing the above is the fact that the Pharisees and the Sadducees, demanding a sign from heaven from the Lord, demanded a miracle similar in character to the [future] antichrist's miracles. The fact that they demanded this particular miracle explains our Lord's reaction to their demand. On hearing such a demand, the God man expressed a deep concern, decisively refused the demand, and did not wish to remain any longer with those who allowed themselves to make such a demand, He departed from them. At another time, He gave the following most stern response, saying *A wicked and adulterous generation seeketh after a sign; and there shall no sign be given unto it, but the sign of the prophet Jonas* (Matt. 16:4). By the words "this generation" are named all who demanded a sign similar in spirit to those described above. They are called "an adulterous generation", because they have entered in spirit into union with satan, breaking their union with God. They are called an adulterous generation because, while recognising the miracles of the God man, they pretended not to see them; demeaning and blaspheming the miracles of God, they asked for a miracle conforming with their sad state of mind and spirit. The request for a sign from heaven was not so much a request for a miracle, but a mockery of the miracles of the God man, and an expression of an ignorant, perverted understanding of miracles. The signs of Jonas the prophet, as explained by the Saviour Himself (Matt. 12:40), were the signs which accompanied His death and resurrection. Then, at the death of Christ, was given God's **sign from heaven**! Then the sun, seeing the Lord crucified, darkened at precisely noon, an all encompassing darkness fell, which lasted for three hours, the veil of the Temple was rent apart by itself from top to bottom, an earthquake occurred, stones were shattered, graves opened, and many saints were resurrected and appeared in the holy city (Luke 23:45; Matt. 27:45, 51 53).

At the Resurrection, again an earthquake occurred. A light bearing angel came down from heaven to the Lord's sepulchre as a witness to the Resurrection, striking with awe the soldiers who were placed at the tomb by those who sought signs from heaven (Matt. 28:2, 3, 11 15). The soldiers told about the Resurrection of the Lord to the Jewish Sanhedrin. Having received a sign from heaven, the Sanhedrin expressed disdain and hatred towards it, as it had expressed towards all the preceding miracles of the God man, proceeding to bribe the soldiers and taking care to cover God's miracle with the darkness of deceit.

Let us turn now to an examination of the miracles done by our Lord Jesus Christ. They are a divine gift to humanity. The gift was not given out of necessity, but solely out of good will and mercy. Men should have approached the gift with the greatest reverence and prudence, for the Bestower of the gift declared Himself God, Who became man for their salvation. The gift was His witness, and had an undisputable value.

The acceptance of salvation is left to man's free will; so also it was left to men to assess the miracles of Christ, to discuss their authenticity and quality, and to draw conclusions from the miracles concerning the One Who did them. The recognition and acceptance of the Redeemer was the result of a free, positive conclusion, not a hurried, light minded action, as if it were a forced attraction. The miracles of Christ had a definite purpose. It can be said concerning all the miracles that which the Lord said to the Apostle Thomas, *Reach hither thy finger, and behold My hands; and reach hither thy hand, and thrust it into My side: and be not faithless, but believing* (John 20:27). The miracles of Christ were tangible, they were clear to the simplest of people, there was nothing mysterious about them, there was no room for doubt or perplexity as to whether it was a miracle or only an effect. The dead were resurrected, the incurably sick were cured, the lepers were cleansed, the blind from birth could see, the dumb could speak, food was multiplied immediately for the needy, the waves of the sea and the wind calmed at a command, those who were threatened by death from the storm were saved, the nets of the fishermen, who laboured in vain for a long time at their task, suddenly filled with fish, obedient to the silent voice of the Lord. The miracles of the God man had many witnesses, among whom were many either hostile to Him or inattentive, or sought from Him only physical help. The miracles were undeniable. The most spiteful enemies of the Lord did not deny them and tried only to demean them by a blasphemous misinterpretation and all means suggested to them by cunning and malice. The miracles of the Lord contained no vanity, no pretence. Not one miracle was done as a display before man; all miracles were covered by the cloak of divine humility. They comprised a chain of blessed benefits for suffering humanity, and at the same time, they expressed totally the power of the Creator over earthly creation and created spirits. They expressed and gave proof to the worthiness of God, Who had taken humanity upon Himself, appearing as a man amid mankind.

One of the Lord's miracles, having a mystical meaning, was not accompanied by a visible benefit for any particular person, but signified a benefit to be poured out on all mankind. The miracle was the withering of the barren fig tree, rich only in leaves (Mark 11:13,14,20). This tree is mentioned in the Scriptures (Gen. 3:7), in the narrative of the fall of our forefathers, as one of the trees of Paradise. It served to cover their nakedness with its leaves, which the forefathers did not notice before falling into sin, a nakedness which sin revealed to them. It may be that the fruit of the fig tree in Paradise was the forbidden fruit. The Lord did not find any fruit on the fig tree. He sought the fruit before its time, letting His flesh seek an untimely desire for food, which mirrors the wrongfulness of the desire of the forefathers; which, as with all the weaknesses of man, the Lord carried upon Himself and destroyed by Himself. Not finding fruit, the Lord rejected the leaves, destroyed the very existence of the tree, at the same time that another tree, the tree of the Cross, was already being prepared as the instrument for the salvation of mankind. The tree, an instrument for the destruction of man, is slain by the command of the Saviour of men. The mystical miracle is accomplished in the presence of only the holy Apostles, the disciples of the mystical teaching. It is accomplished before the very entry of the God man upon the struggle of His atoning suffering for mankind, before being lifting up on the Cross.

The miracles of the Lord had a holy meaning, a holy goal. Although they in themselves were a great benefit in the dispensation of God's plan, they served as witness and proof of an immensely higher benevolence. In becoming man, the Lord brought to humanity an eternal, spiritual, priceless gift salvation, healing from sin, resurrection from eternal death.

The word of the Lord and His life were the realisation of this all-encompassing gift, in His life the Lord was without sin, all holy (John 8:46); His word was filled with power (Mark 1:42). Men had fallen deeply into the darkness and gloom of carnal mindedness [versus spiritual mindedness]; their hearts and minds were blinded. It was necessary for special condescension towards the ailing condition of men, it became necessary to give the most clear witness to their physical senses, it became necessary by means of physical senses to impart a life giving knowledge to minds and hearts, which through their natural death died an eternal death. Miracles are given to support the Word of God. For man to understand and accept the spiritual gift, seen only by spiritual eyes, the Lord added to the spiritual, eternal gift one similar to it, a gift which was temporal, bodily the healing of man's bodily illnesses. Sin is the cause of all illnesses in man, both spiritual and bodily, it serves as the cause of temporary and eternal death. In showing His power over the consequences of sin in the body of man, the Lord shows His power over sin itself. The carnal understanding does not perceive illnesses of the spirit, nor eternal death, but it sees and accepts bodily illnesses; they impress and concern it very much. The Lord healed all the sick with one word, one command, resurrected the dead, expelled unclean spirits, showed His Power. He showed the power of God over man, over sin, over fallen spirits, and He showed this openly to our physical senses, to the carnal mind. This carnal mind, seeing and touching this power, could and should have logically acknowledged the power of the Lord over sin not only in relation to sin of body, but in the relation to sin of the soul, and acknowledge the power of the Lord over the soul itself. In some miracles of the Lord, as in the resurrection of the dead, the unlimited divine power was shown over the body and the soul. The body quickened, the soul was called back into it, having already departed to the world of spirits. It was called from that world and united with the body, from which it had separated forever. Man received signs within himself, not out of himself. Man was given proof of salvation in himself, not from a distance. The witness for eternal salvation of soul and body was given through a temporal salvation of the body from bodily ills and bodily death. With correct and devout observation of the miracles of the Lord, they prove to be filled with divine reason. A demand for a sign from heaven is shown to be devoid of sense. Although it was rare that the power of the Lord extended beyond man onto the matter of created nature, these occurrences did take place. They witness to the fact that the power of the Lord over all of nature is the unlimited power of God. The miracles over nature serve to complement those miracles which were performed for mankind, so that the significance that mankind was wont to give to the One Who redeemed our sins was accurately defined. Since the reason for our Lord's coming to earth was the salvation of man, the care of the Lord was concentrated on man, the most perfect creation His image, His rational temple. The earth, the land of exile, suffering, and our journeying, all material creation, despite its immensity, is left by Him without attention. Even if certain miracles are performed on matter, they are done for the satisfaction of man's needs.

Such is the significance of the miracles performed by the Lord and His Apostles. This was made clear by the Lord to the Apostles. Once, a multitude gathered in the house where the Lord was present. The house was filled and the crowd was pressing, it was impossible to enter. At this time, a paralytic was brought, who could not leave his bed. Those who brought him, seeing the multitude and the pressing of the crowd, took the sick man up onto the roof, made an opening in the ceiling, and let him down on his bed before the Lord. Seeing their act of faith, the merciful Lord said to the paralytic, *Son, thy sins be forgiven thee.* Here sat some of the scribes, who knew the law to the letter, but infected by envy towards the God man, immediately thought that blasphemy was uttered. *Why doth this man thus speak blasphemies? who can forgive sins but God only?* The One to Whom all hearts are open, said to them, *Why reason ye these things in your hearts? Whether is it easier to say to the sick of the palsy, Thy sins be forgiven thee; or to say, Arise, and take up thy bed, and walk? But that ye may know that the Son of man hath power on earth to forgive sins, (He saith to the sick of the palsy,) I say unto thee, arise, and take up thy bed, and go thy way into thine house* (Mark 2:2 11). To say without proof that "your sins are forgiven" can be done by a hypocrite and a deceiver. The paralytic was healed immediately and became strong, took up the bed and walked before all present. The miracle is filled with divine wisdom and goodness. Initially the Lord grants the ailing, suffering being, a spiritual gift, unseen by physical eyes the remission of sins.

The granting of this gift gave rise to an involuntary confession by the learned Jewish men, that such a gift can be granted only by God. The Lord, answering the thought in their hearts, gives them a new testimony of Himself, that He is God. Finally, the spiritual gift and spiritual proof are sealed with a material gift and proof the immediate and full recovery of the sick man. The holy Evangelist Mark, concluding his Gospel, says that the Apostles, upon the Ascension of the Lord, preached the Word everywhere, while the Lord worked with them, and confirmed the message by signs (Mark 16:20).

This thought was expressed by all the Apostles in the prayer through which they had recourse to God after the threats by the Sanhedrin, which forbade them to teach and act in the name of Jesus: *And now, Lord, behold their threatenings: and grant unto Thy servants, that with all boldness they may speak Thy word, by stretching forth Thine hand to heal; and that signs and wonders may be done by the name of Thy holy child Jesus* (Acts 4:29 30).

The signs of God were given to assist the word of God. They were a witness to the power and significance of the word (Luke 4:36). The essential agent is the Word. Signs are not needed where the word is accepted, because the worthiness of the word is understood. Signs are a condescension to human weakness.

The word acts in one manner, the signs act in another. The words act directly on the mind and heart, the signs on the mind and heart through the senses. The consequences of the action of the word are stronger, more powerful, more definite than the consequences from the action of the signs.

When the word and the signs act together, then the action of the signs is left as if unnoticed, by reason of the abundant action of the word. This is clear from the narrative in the Gospel. Nicodemus was influenced by the signs, and he recognised in the Lord only a teacher sent by God (John 3:2). The Apostle Peter was influenced by the word and he confessed the Lord as the Christ, the Son of God. *Thou hast the words of eternal life,* he said to the God man, *and we believe and are sure that Thou art that Christ, the Son of the Living God* (John 6:68 69). The holy Peter was an eyewitness of the many miracles of the Lord. The multiplication of the five loaves and the feeding of a large gathering of people had just been performed by the Lord, but the Apostle at his confession is silent about the miracles and speaks only of the power and the action of the words. The same happened with the two disciples, who conversed with the Lord on the way to Emmaus without recognising Him. Upon coming to the town, already in the house, at the breaking of the bread, they recognised Him. Just as they recognised the Lord, He became invisible. They did not say anything about the amazing miracle, they turned all their attention to the action of the word: *Did not our heart burn within* us, they said to each other, *while He talked with us by the way, and while He opened to us the scriptures* (Luke 24:32)?

The God man blessed the ones who did not see the signs, and who believed (John 20:29). He expressed sympathy towards those who, not satisfied with the word, needed miracles: *Except ye see signs and wonders ye will not believe,* He said to the nobleman of Capernaum (John 4:48).

It is so! Worthy of sympathy are those who forsake the word, who seek affirmation from miracles. This need is derived from the predominance of the carnal mind, a coarse ignorance, a way of life brought as an offering to corruption and sin, a lack of exercise in the study of the Law of God and in God pleasing virtues, an inability of the soul to feel the Holy Spirit, to perceive the presence of the Holy Spirit in the Word. Signs were designated most of all for convincing and bringing to faith those who were still of a carnal mind, occupied by the sentient cares of the world. Immersed in the concerns of life, always attached with their soul to earth and its affairs, and little able to value the merit of the word, the merciful Word drew them to salvation given through the word, by means of visible signs, which contained a material affirmation acting through the senses, bringing a weak soul to the almighty, saving word. Those who believed on account of signs made up a lower category of believers in Christ. When they were offered a spiritual most elevated, all holy teaching, then many understood it according to their own interpretation (John 6:60), and did not wish to ask for an explanation of God's word, which was spirit and life. They were convicted by the superficial witness of their heart, and many fell away (John 6:66).

Neither the signs, nor the word of the God man acted beneficially on the Jewish high priests, scribes, Pharisees and Sadducees, though, with the exception of the latter, they knew precisely to the letter, the law of God. They were not only alien to God and full of enmity towards God on account of a sinful ailment common to all mankind, but became thus confirmed and sealed themselves in such a state on account of their own wilfulness, on account of self conceit, on account of a desire to lead that life and be successful in that life which was forbidden by the Gospel.

They would not hear the Son of God speaking to them. They did not hear His words as they should. They did not hearken to Him, but only caught those words which seemed to them necessary for misinterpreting and accusing the Lord. So hate is developed for the words of the one who is hated. *Why do ye not understand My speech? Even because ye cannot hear My word* (John 8:43), the Saviour would say to His enemies, who denied stubbornly and with obstinacy the salvation offered to them. Why do you not understand My teaching? Why do you not accept My healing Word? Because you cannot even hear My words, it is unbearable to you. Being the children of lies and acting in this manner, you do not believe Me. *And because I tell you the truth, ye believe Me not* (John 8:45). *He that is of God heareth God's words: ye therefore hear them not, because ye are not from God* (John 8:47). *If I do not the works of My Father, believe Me not. But if I do, though ye believe not Me, believe the works: that ye may know, and believe, that the Father is in Me, and I am in Him* (John 10:37 38). In vain were those words, which being the truth of God, comprised a full witness (John 8:14). In vain the miracles, which were in themselves a full witness, so tangible and obvious, that the enemies of the God man, in all their desire and effort to deny them, could not help but recognise them (John 9:24).

The means which acted upon those who did not know the law of God, who were not well acquainted with it, who spent their lives in earthly occupations and concerns, but did not wilfully deny the law of God, this same means had no influence on those who knew the law of God in detail and to the letter, but denied it in their lives and their wilfulness (John 5:46 47; 7:19). All that could be done for the salvation of men was done by the ineffable mercy of God. The Saviour makes clear, *If I had not come and spoken unto them, they had not had sin: but now they have no cloak for their sin. He that hateth Me hateth My Father also. If I had not done among them the works which no other man did, they had not had sin: but now have they both seen and hated both Me and My Father* (John 15: 22 24).

Christianity was brought to us so perfectly that there is no justification for those who do not know it. The reason for lack of knowledge is only wilfulness. As the sun shines from the heavens, so shines Christianity. One who wilfully closes one's eyes, must credit his lack of sight to his own wilfulness and not to the lack of light.

The reason for mankind's denial of the God man is in men. Also in man is the reason for the acceptance of antichrist. *I am come in My Father's name, and ye receive Me not: if another shall come in his own name, him ye will receive* (John 5:43). They are both named as denying Christ and accepting the antichrist, though the antichrist is spoken of as one who is to come. The denial of Christ comes from man's spirit, and the same spirit accepts the antichrist. They [those who denied Christ then] were added to those who accepted antichrist, though they completed their earthly journey many centuries before his coming. They accomplished his [the antichrist's] greatest misdeed the killing of God. A crime similar to deicide was not left for the time of antichrist. As their spirit was in a state of enmity towards Christ, so it was in the state of union with the antichrist, though separated from him by a great span of time, now reaching to the end of the second millennium.

And every spirit that confesseth not that Jesus Christ is come in the flesh is not of God: and this is that spirit of antichrist, whereof ye have heard that it should come; and even now already is it in the world (I John 4:3), says the Theologian. Those led by the spirit of the antichrist deny Christ, they have accepted the antichrist in their spirit, entered into union with him, subordinated and worshipped him in spirit, confessing him as their god. *And for this cause God shall send them strong delusion,* (that is, God will allow it), *that they should believe a lie: that they all might be damned who believed not the Truth, but had pleasure in unrighteousness* (II Thess. 2:11 12). In this judgement God is just. This will satisfy as well as accuse and judge the human spirit. The antichrist will come in his own, foreordained time. His coming will be preceded by a universal apostasy in most men from the Christian faith. Through apostasy from Christ, mankind will prepare itself for the acceptance of the antichrist, it will accept him in its spirit. In the very mood of the human spirit there will arise a demand, an invitation for the antichrist, a sympathy for him, as in a serious illness there arises a thirst for a poisonous draught. The invitation is pronounced! A beckoning voice is heard in society, expressing an insistent need for the genius of geniuses, who would raise material development and success to the highest degree, who would usher on earth such material well being, that heaven and earth will become superfluous for man. The antichrist will be a logical, equitable, natural result of the common moral and spiritual direction of man.

The miracles of the incarnate God comprised the greatest material blessings which mankind could imagine. What blessing could be more precious than a return to life of one who died? What blessing could be more precious than the healing of an incurable illness, which was taking away one's life, making life a slow dying rather than living? However, despite the beneficence, holiness, spiritual significance of the miracles of Christ, these miracles were only temporal gifts. To define them exactly, they should be called signs. They were signs of the word for eternal salvation. Those who were resurrected by the God man died in their time, for they were granted only an extension to their earthly life and were not given this life forever. Healed by the God man, they again became ill and died; health was given to them only for a time, but not forever. The temporal and material benefits were poured out as a sign of eternal and spiritual benefits, so that they would believe in the existence of unseen gifts and would accept them. The signs delivered them from the abyss of ignorance and sensuality and led them to faith; faith imparted knowledge of eternal blessings and taught the desire to acquire them. With the help of wondrous signs the Apostles swiftly spread Christianity throughout the world: the signs were a clear and powerful witness of Christianity for the educated nations, for those who still dwelt in spiritual ignorance and barbarism. When faith was planted everywhere, the word was planted, then the signs were taken away, having completed their service. They ceased to act everywhere. They were performed sometimes by the elect holy ones of God. Saint John Chrysostom, church father and writer of the fourth and fifth centuries, says that already in his time, the action of the signs of Grace had ceased, although they still occurred in some places, especially among the monastics, the standard bearers of signs. In the course of time, these standard bearers became fewer. The holy Fathers foretold about the last times, when standard bearing men will be no more.

"Why, say some, are there no signs now? My answer to that is, listen with special attention, because the question asked here I hear from many, and often, and always. Why at that time all who accepted baptism, started to speak in foreign tongues and now this does not happen? Why now is the Grace of miracles taken away from men? God accomplishes this not to subject us to dishonour but gives us an even greater honour. In what manner? I will explain. People of those times were slower of mind, as they were only just turned away from idols. Their minds were carnal and dull, they were immersed in the material and given over to it, they could not realise the existence of immaterial gifts. Neither did they know the meaning of spiritual Grace, that all is accepted by faith alone, and for this reason they were given signs. Of the spiritual gifts some are unseen and are accepted only by faith, others are conjoined with some sign, subject to the senses, for the arousal of belief in the unbelieving. For example, the remission of sins is a spiritual gift and it is unseen we do not see by our bodily eyes how our sins are being cleansed. The soul is being cleansed, but the soul is invisible to the eyes of the body. And thus the cleansing of sins is a spiritual gift, which cannot be visible by the eyes of the body; the ability to speak in foreign tongues, although part of the action of the Spirit, serves with It as a sign, subject to the senses, and thus can be easily observed by the unbelievers an unseen action which is accomplished in the soul become seen and is shown by means of external language, which we hear. For this same reason, Paul says: *But the manifestation of the Spirit is given to every man to profit withal* (I Cor. 12:7).

And thus, I do not have need of signs. Why is it? Because I have learnt to believe in the Grace of God without the signs. An unbeliever is in need of proof, but I am a believer, and have no need whatsoever in proof or a sign. Although I do not speak in tongues, but I know that I am cleansed of sin. The former did not believe until they received a sign. Signs were given to them as a proof of faith, which they were accepting. And so signs were given not to believers, but to the unbelieving so that they would be made believers, in the words of Paul, *for a sign not to them that believe, but to them that believe not* (I Cor. 14:22). (First Homily of Saint John Chrysostom at Pentecost)

If signs were absolutely necessary, they would have remained. The word remained and signs were part of its installation. The word spread, came to reign, encompassed the universe. It is fully explained by the Fathers of the Church, made available and easy to understand. It is absolutely necessary, it grants eternal blessings, it accomplishes man's salvation. It brings the heavenly kingdom, it preserves the spiritual, most elevated signs of God (Ps. 118:18), *But the word of the Lord endureth forever* (I Peter 1:25). In the Word is life, and It is life (John 1:4). It gives birth to eternal life for those who died, granting to them from within Itself Its all holy life: the hearers and doers of the Word are those *being born again, not of corruptible seed, but of incorruptible, by the word* of *God, which liveth and abideth forever* (I Peter 1:23). To understand the significance of the word, we must fulfil it. The commandments of the Gospel which are being fulfilled immediately start to transform, change, enliven man, his mode of thought, the feelings of his heart, his very body. *For the word of God is quick, and powerful, and sharper than any two edged sword, piercing even to the dividing asunder of soul and spirit, and of the joints and marrow, and is a discerner of the thoughts and intents* of *the heart* (Heb. 4:12).

The word of God contains in itself its [own] witness. Similar to healing signs, it acts in the man himself, and by this action witnesses of itself. It is the highest sign. It is a spiritual sign, which being granted to man, satisfies all needs for his salvation and makes the concurrence from material signs unnecessary. A Christian who does not know the attributes of the word, denounces himself as being cold towards the word, ignorant of the word of God, or only possessing dead knowledge according to the letter alone.

Part II

The desire of contemporary Christian society to see miracles and even to perform miracles must not be ignored. This desire must be thoroughly scrutinised since the desire to perform miracles is severely condemned by the Holy Fathers. Through such a desire, self delusion, which is based on conceit and vanity and which lives in and possesses the soul, manifests itself. The great instructor of monks, Saint Isaac of Syria, discusses this matter: "The Lord is a close defender of His saints at all times; but, without need, He does not manifest His power through a visible act or a sensory sign, in order that His defence not become commonplace for us and that we should not lose proper reverence towards Him. This loss of reverence would cause harm to us. Thus He acts through His Providence for the saints. In every circumstance He allows them to struggle in conformance to their strength and to their labour in prayers. He also shows them that His secret care for them does not cease for even a moment. If the circumstance by its difficulty surpasses their reason, if they will lose strength and will not be able to act within their natural limitations, then He Himself will accomplish that which is needed for their help, in the majesty of His power, and as He deems right. He strengthens them when possible in secret, giving them the strength to overcome their sorrow. He resolves a complex sorrow with wisdom which He imparts, and the knowledge of His Providence leads to praise, beneficial in all respects. When the circumstance demands visible help, then by necessity He does this too. His means and manner of assistance are most wise. They help in poverty, in necessity, and do not act without reason. One who dares and asks God to accomplish something unusual, while not being pressed by necessity, one who desires that miracles and signs would be accomplished by his hands, is tempted in his mind by the devil, who is mocking him, and that person is seen as vain and ailing in his conscience. It is right in one's sorrow to ask for Divine help, but to tempt God without need is disastrous. Most unrighteous is the one who wishes it. In the lives of the saints we find examples where the Lord, expressing His disapproval would fulfil such desires. One who wants and desires this on his own, not being pressed, falls from the condition of spiritual self-preservation and in this state departs from the mind of truth. If the one who asks is heard, then the Evil One finds a place in him, like in a person who walks before God without reverence, with insolence. The devil then plunges him into greater audacity. The truly righteous ones not only do not desire to be miracle workers, but even when they are given the gift of miracle-working, decline it. Not only do they not wish it before the eyes of men, but also in the secret chambers of their heart. One of the holy fathers, because of his purity, received by the Grace of God a divine gift to discern the thoughts of those who came to him. He asked God and begged his friends to pray that this gift would be taken from him. If some saints accepted the gift, they accepted it out of necessity, or by reason of their simplicity; others accepted it never without reason through the instruction of the divine Spirit acting in them. Truly righteous ones constantly consider themselves to be unworthy before God. The fact that they consider themselves accursed and not worthy of the care of God, witnesses to their truth" (Homily 36, according to the translation by Elder Paisius).

From these holy reflections the conclusion can be drawn that those who wish to perform signs, wish to do so due to the excitement of the flesh, attracted by the passions which they misunderstand, although it may seem to them that they are led by zeal for God's work. Those who seek signs are in a similar condition of excitement and self delusion. It is forbidden in all circumstances to tempt God and to cease revering Him. It is permitted to ask for God's help in extreme need, when we have no means of our own to be delivered from it, but determining the means of assistance we must leave to God, committing ourselves to His will and mercy. The Lord always sends means for assistance which will be helpful to the soul. The means offer the help we are in need of, and in that very assistance He grants us a holy taste of humility.

Divine help does not occur with outward brilliance, as our carnal mind might wish, so that the soul will not be harmed from the vainglory of being satisfied with this brilliance. In the works of God, in the very service to the Church, one should always ask for the blessing of God and the help of God. One must believe that only divine, spiritual means can be beneficial for faith and devotion, but never the means suggested by the carnal mind.

It is difficult for man to endure glory without harm to his soul (Saint Isaac of Syria, Homily 1). It is difficult not only for the passionate or those struggling with passions, but also for those who have conquered the passions and for saints. Although victory over sin has been granted to them, changeability has not been taken from them, that is, the possibility of returning to sin and falling under the yoke of the passions. This has happened to some who were not attentive enough to themselves, who allowed self assurance to slip in concerning their spiritual condition. As the blessed Macarius the Great (Conversation VII, ch. 4) noted, an inclination to pride dwells in even the most cleansed souls. This very inclination acts as the beginning of going astray and attraction [to passion]. Because of this, the gift of healing and other visible gifts are very dangerous for those to whom they are given, as they are highly valued by carnal and sensuous people, and are glorified by them. The unseen, blessed gifts, incomparably higher than the ones seen, such as the gift to lead souls to salvation and to heal them from the passions, are not understood or seen by the world. The world not only does not glorify the servants of God who have these gifts, but persecutes them as ones acting against the powers of the world, as casting aspersions on the dominion of the prince of the world (Saint Tikhon of Zadonsk, Vol.15, letter 103. sect. 4). The merciful God grants men that which is essential and useful, although they do not understand or value it. He does not grant that which is of little use, and often may be quite harmful, although carnal understanding and ignorance insatiably thirst for it and seek it.

"Many," says Isaac of Syria, "performed signs, resurrected the dead, laboured in the conversion of the lost, performed great miracles, and after this, they themselves, who had given life to others, fell into evil and the abomination of passions and gave themselves over to death" (Homily 56). Blessed Macarius the Great tells us that a certain ascetic who lived near him received the gift of healing in such abundance that he would heal the sick with just the laying on of hands, but being glorified by men, he became proud and fell into the very depth of sin (Conversation XXVII, ch.16). In the Life of the venerable Anthony the Great, a certain young monk is mentioned who ruled over wild beasts in the desert. When the great one heard of this miracle he expressed distrust in the spiritual condition of the miracle worker. Not long after word came of the grievous fall of the monk *(Alphabetical Patericon).* In the fourth century there lived in Egypt a certain elder who had the special gift of miracles, and because of it, great glory among men. Soon he noticed that pride started to possess him and that he was not able to vanquish it through his own efforts. The elder turned to God with the warmest of prayers beseeching Him that he would be allowed to become possessed in order to achieve humility. God fulfilled this humble request of His servant and allowed satan to enter him. The elder submitted to all the attacks of possession for over five months; he had to be chained. The people who came to him in multitudes, who glorified him as a great saint, left him, making it known that he had lost his mind. The elder, who was now freed from the glory of men and from his pride, which had started to grow in him because of this glory, thanked God Who saved him from destruction. His salvation was accomplished by means of a short term difficulty and dishonour before carnal men, who did not understand that because of the sign, the devil inflicted a trial on the elder, and that by means of visible possession the elder was returned to the safe path by the wondrous mercy of God *(Patrologiae L. LXXIII.* De vitis patrum, lib. IV, ch. XIII). Thus it becomes clear why the great fathers such as Sisoes, Pimen and others, having the most generous gift of healing, tried to hide it. They did not trust themselves, they realised man's capacity to easily change, and instead through humility kept themselves from spiritual misfortune *(Alphabetical Patericon)*. The holy Apostles, who were given the gift of miracles to accompany their preaching, were allowed by the Providence of God to bear heavy sorrows and persecutions, with the aim of keeping them from pride. Saint Isaac of Syria says, "A gift without temptation is the destruction of the soul for those who accept it. If your deed is acceptable to God, and He grants you a gift, then beg Him to grant you the knowledge of how to be humble with such a gift, or that you might have protection with this gift (the misfortunes permitted were just such a guard of the gift for the holy Apostles), or that the gift might be taken away from you if it becomes the cause of your ruin, for not all can keep riches without harm to themselves" (Homily 34).

The attitude of the spiritually minded with respect to the ills of the body and the miraculous healing of them is completely different from the view of a carnally minded person. The carnal mind considers illnesses a misfortune and their healing, especially a miraculous one, as the greatest good, little caring whether the healing is joined with benefit to the soul or its harm. The spiritual mind even sees in illness sent by divine Providence the mercy of God towards man. Enlightened by the light of God's Word spiritual reason teaches conduct pleasing to God and salvific for the soul. It teaches that it is possible to seek and ask God for the healing of an illness, with the firm intent to use the return of good health and strength to serve God, but not to the service of vanity and sin. In the latter case the miraculous healing will lead only to greater condemnation and will bring a more severe punishment in the present and for all eternity. This was witnessed by the Lord. Having healed the paralytic He told him, *Behold, thou art made whole: sin no more, lest a worse thing come unto thee* (John 5:14). Man is weak and easily inclined towards sin. If some saints who had the blessed gift of healing and were abundantly endowed with spiritual reasoning succumbed to temptation from sin and fell, how much easier is it for carnal people, lacking a proper understanding of spiritual gifts, to abuse the divine gift. And many did abuse it! Having received healing from an illness in a miraculous way, they did not pay attention to the divine Grace of God and their obligation to be thankful for that Grace. They started to lead a sinful life, turning the gift of God into harm for themselves, alienating themselves from God and losing their salvation. Because of this, miraculous healings of physical illnesses occur rarely, although the carnal mind very much respects and desires them. *Ye ask, and receive not,* says the Apostle, *because ye ask amiss, that ye may consume it upon your lusts* (James 4:3). A spiritual mind learns that ailments and other sorrows, which God allows for men, can be sent by a particular divine mercy; as bitter medicines for the ill, they help us work towards our salvation, our eternal happiness, far more surely than miraculous healings. Often, quite often, the ailment is a greater Grace than would be a healing if it were to come; the ailment can be a favour so essential that its removal through healing would be the taking away of a great good, incomparable with that temporal benefit which is given by the healing of a bodily ailment. The ailing beggar Lazarus, spoken of in the Gospel, was not healed from a burdensome illness, nor freed from poverty, ending his years in those circumstances in which he suffered for a long time but for his patience he was taken by the angels to the bosom of Abraham (see Luke 16:22).

The Holy Scriptures affirm that without exception all the saints of God completed their earthly journey along a narrow and thorny path, filled with various sorrows and deprivations (Hebrews 12). Based on such understanding of sorrows, true servants of God, in their attitude towards the sorrows which befell them, conducted themselves with great wisdom and self denial. They met the sorrow which came, whatever it was, as something that belonged to them (Saint Mark the Ascetic, *226 Chapters on Those Who Think to be Justified by Deeds,* ch. 6). They believed with all their soul that such sorrow would not come if it were not allowed by the just and all good God, according to man's needs. Their first act when sorrow came was to acknowledge that they deserved it. They sought and always found in themselves the reason for sorrow. Then if they noted that their sorrow was an impediment for them in pleasing God, they would turn with prayer to God for the deliverance from this sorrow, leaving the fulfilment or non fulfilment of their request to the will of God, never considering their own understanding of the sorrow to be correct. One's judgement cannot be totally correct, for the judgement of a limited, though holy person, does not encompass and perceive all the reasons for the sorrow as it is encompassed and perceived by the all seeing eye of God, Who allows sorrows to befall His servants and His beloved. The holy Apostle Paul thrice turned with prayer to God, asking that the messenger of satan, who impeded the Apostle in the preaching of Christianity, would be removed. Paul was not hearkened to, the judgement of God on this matter was other than that of the God inspired Apostle (II Cor. 12:7 10). The surrender of oneself to the will of God, a sincere, reverent desire that it might be manifested in us, is the necessary, natural consequence of true, spiritual reasoning. Holy monks, when they were subject to illness, accepted it as the greatest Grace of God, and tried to remain in a state of glorifying and giving thanks to God, not seeking healing. Miraculous healings, however, happen most often among holy monks. They desired to patiently and humbly suffer that which God allowed, believing and confessing that it is better for the soul than all self willed ascetic acts. Blessed Pimen the Great said, "Three monastic deeds are equal in worth when one remains truly silent, when one is ill and thanks God, and when one goes through obedience with pure thoughts" *(Alphabetical Patericon).*

In the Egyptian Skete, where the greatest of holy monks lived, there lived the blessed Benjamin. For his virtuous life God granted him a rich gift of healing. Having the gift he himself submitted to a burdensome and lengthy illness of dropsy. He became heavy in body and they had to take him out of his cell to another, more spacious one. To do that they had to remove the doors and door jambs. In his new cell a special seat was made for him because he could not lie on a bed. In this position the ailing monk continued to heal others, and those who saw his suffering sympathised with him. He taught them that they should pray for his soul, and not be concerned about his body. "For when my body is well," he said, "then I do not have much benefit from it. Now, enduring an illness, it does not bring me any harm." *(Alphabetical Patericon)*

Abba Peter said that he once visited the venerable Isaiah the Recluse and found him suffering from a painful illness. As he expressed sympathy, the venerable one said, "I am overwhelmed by illness, yet I can barely preserve the memory of the awesome time (of death and the judgement of God). If my body were healthy, then the remembrance of this would be totally alien to me. When the body is healthy, then it is inclined to hostile acts against God. Sorrows serve us as an aid in keeping God's commandments (Venerable Isaiah the Recluse, Homily 27). The holy fathers, when overtaken by illness or some other sorrow, at first tried to show patience, which depended on them. They had recourse to self reproach and self-judgement, thus forcing their heart and compelling it to patience (Abba Dorotheos, Instruction 7). They remembered death, the judgement of God, and eternal torment; such remembrance weakens the significance and feeling of earthly sorrows (Matt. 10:28 31). They raised their minds to God's Providence, reminding themselves of the promise of the Son of God to always be with His followers and preserve them. With this in mind they summoned their hearts to blessed peacefulness and courage (Matt. 28:20). They compelled themselves to glorify and thank God for the sorrow, and forced themselves to be conscious of their sinfulness, which demanded punishment and proper understanding, because of God's justice, and His goodness. While forcing themselves to labour for patience, they increased their diligent prayers to God to grant a spiritual gift blessed patience, inseparable from another spiritual gift—blessed humility, which together serve the faithful as a pledge of salvation and eternal blessedness. The great standard bearing fathers did not grant healing, as much as it was possible for them, to their disciples who were subjected by the will or Providence of God to illness, so as not to deprive them of spiritual profit, which would without fail be given, according to the moral tradition of the Church, through the bearing of illness and suffering. The abbot of a monastery in Gaza, blessed Serid, the disciple of the great Barsanuphius, who was a hermit living in silence in the same monastery, was ill for a long time. Some of the elder brothers asked the great one for the healing of the abbot. The holy Barsanuphius answered, "Some of the holy ones living here could pray for the health of my son, and I advised him of it, and he would not be ill for one day, but then he would not receive the fruits of patience. This illness is beneficial to him for patience and thanksgiving" (Answer 130). Explaining the necessity of sorrows for an ascetic of Christ, Saint Isaac of Syria says, "Temptation is beneficial for every man. If it is beneficial to Paul, then *every mouth may be stopped, and all the world may become guilty before God* (Rom. 3:19). The ascetics are subject to temptations so that they might increase their wealth; weak ones to keep themselves from that which is harmful for them; sleeping ones so that they would awake; those standing afar, to come closer to God; His own, to become more of His own. An untaught son does not come to manage his father's wealth, for he will not be able to manage it well. Because of this, God allows temptation at first and wearies one, and then grants the gift. Glory to the Master, Who with bitter medicines gives us the delight of health. There is no man who does not grieve during his instruction, no man, to whom the time does not appear bitter when he drinks the draught of temptations. But without them it is impossible to become spiritually strong. And to endure is not in our power. How can a clay vessel carry fine water if beforehand it is not strengthened by Divine fire? If, with reverence and an unceasing desire for patience, we will humbly ask God for it, then we will receive all from Christ Jesus, our Lord" (Homily 37).

Part III (Conclusion)

Before the Second Coming of Christ *there shall be signs in the sun, and in the moon, and in the stars* (Luke 21:25), the sea will roar and be tossed. How are we to discern these signs from the signs of the Antichrist, as he also will give signs in the sun and moon, the stars and air *(Commentary on the Gospel of Mark by Blessed Theophylact,* 8:11 12)? The first signs will be true and thus they will be completely different from the signs of the Antichrist, which will be comprised of manifestations deceiving the senses. The performers of the signs of the Antichrist will be the Antichrist and his apostles; the signs in the sun, moon and stars, these signs heralds of the coming of Christ, will appear by themselves, without any intermediary. The heavenly lights will have fulfilled their designation for which, by the command of their Creator, they came to shine in the heavens (Gen. 1:14). They fulfilled their assignment (significance) at the Birth of Christ, through a miraculous star (Matt. 2:2), they fulfilled it at the crucifixion of the God man, when the sun was covered by a thick cover of darkness at noon-time (Matt. 27:45). The Holy Evangelist Matthew tells us that upon the cessation of sorrows, produced by the reign of the Antichrist, the coming of Christ will occur immediately and it will begin with [the signs when] *the sun shall be darkened, and the moon shall not give her light, and the stars shall fall from heaven* (Matt. 24:29). These celestial bodies will remain in their places, notes the blessed Theophylact of Bulgaria, but they will dim and will appear to one's eyes as having disappeared from the vault of heaven, because of the abundance of heavenly light, filling the world in preparation for the acceptance of the Lord in His glory.

We are emboldened to call our teaching on miracles and signs the expression of the Holy Fathers. The necessity of presenting this teaching in an exact and detailed exposition is obvious.

True signs were to assist true knowledge of God, and the salvation it granted. False signs assisted error and the destruction it produced. In particular, the action of the signs produced by the Antichrist will be vast and powerful, it will carry unfortunate mankind to the recognition of the messenger of satan as god. A devout contemplation of the miracles accomplished by our Lord Jesus Christ is edifying and consoling, and acts for the salvation of our souls. What holy simplicity there is in them! These miracles made it so easy to know God. What blessed goodness, what humility, what indisputable force of conviction! The contemplation of Christ's miracles leads us to the Word, Who is God. In order to restore fallen mankind to communion with Him, God blessedly willed that His Word become incarnate and live among men, enter into the closest relation with them, making them His own, and lift them to heaven. Having put on humanity, the Word remains the Word of God, and acts as the Word of God according to Its Divine essence. He sits at the right hand of the Father in His adopted humanity and dwells everywhere as God. It [the Word] is inscribed on paper. It is clothed in on sounds, but being Spirit and Life (John 6:63) It enters minds and hearts, re-establishing those who unite with Him in spirit, and draws the body also to a spiritual life. Contemplating the miracles of Christ, we rise to the knowledge of the awesome significance which is contained in the Word of God. *The one thing needful* (Luke 10:42) for our salvation is the Word which serves salvation and accomplishes salvation with all perfection. Knowing the Word of God from the Holy Scriptures, uttered by the Holy Spirit and explained by the Holy Spirit united with knowledge received from this activity, directed according to the Word of God, blessed by the knowledge given by Divine Grace, grants to the Christian purity of mind and heart. In this purity comes to shine spiritual reasoning, like the sun on a clear, cloudless sky. At the dawn of day after the night's darkness, the images of sensory objects change: some, until then invisible, become visible; others which were seen unclearly, blending with other objects, are now separated from them and become defined. This occurs not because the objects change, but because the relation of human sight towards them changes with the change of the darkness to the light of day. Exactly the same occurs in the relation of the human mind to objects moral and spiritual, when the mind is enlightened by spiritual knowledge proceeding from the Holy Spirit. Only with the light of spiritual reasoning can the soul see the holy way to God! Only with the light of spiritual reasoning can the unseen procession of the mind and heart to God be accomplished without sin. Only with the light of spiritual reasoning can we escape error, the thickets and abyss of destruction. There, where this light is not, there is no sight of truth; there, where this light is not, there is no God pleasing virtue which saves man and leads him into the mansions of paradise (Saint Isaac the Syrian, Homilies 25, 26, 27, & 28).

To avoid the misfortunes into which the viewing of signs and miracles by the carnal mind can entice us, the sight of the spiritual eye should be enlightened with the light of spiritual reasoning. We saw the essence of the miracles accomplished by the God man. We saw what their goal was. The signs, having accomplished their service, departed, leaving now the essential doer the Word to act, Who remains and will remain the doer until the end of the world, as He Himself said of Himself: *I am with you always, even unto the end of the world* (Matt. 28:20).

When the universal signs had ceased, accomplishing the sowing of Christianity by the preaching of the Apostles and those who were Equal to the Apostles, signs were performed in places by the elect vessels of the Holy Spirit. In the course of time, with the gradual weakening of Christianity and the corruption of morality, miracle working men grew fewer (see *The Ladder,* Homily 26, chap. 52). Finally, they ceased completely. In the meantime, men, while losing reverence and respect for all that is sacred, losing humility, acknowledging themselves unworthy not only to accomplish signs, but even to see them, thirst for miracles more than ever before. Humanity, intoxicated with self conceit, presumption and ignorance, strives without discernment, rashly and boldly, towards all that seems miraculous and does not refuse to be a participant in performing miracles, but is determined to do it, without a second thought. Such a thoughtless movement is fraught with more danger than ever before. We are gradually approaching that time when a vast spectacle of numerous and amazing false miracles will be revealed, enticing into destruction those unfortunate children of carnal reasoning, who will be seduced and tricked by these miracles.

The quickening of the soul by the Word of God results in a living faith in Christ. A living faith, as it were, sees Christ (Heb. 11:27). Christianity is revealed before its eyes, while remaining a mystery; while remaining unknowable it is clear and understandable; it is no longer covered by that thick, impenetrable curtain, as when faith is dead. A living faith is spiritual reasoning (Saint Isaac the Syrian, Homily 28). It has no need of signs, being wholly satisfied by the signs of Christ, and the greatest of His signs, the crown of signs His Word. The desire to see signs serves as an indication of unbelief, and the signs were given to unbelievers to turn them to belief. Let us cling to the Word of God with all our soul, let us unite with Him into one spirit, and the signs of the Antichrist will not even attract our attention. With disdain and revulsion we will turn our eyes away from them, as from a demonic spectacle, as from an act of fanatical enemies of God, as from a mocking of God, and as from deathly poison and infection. Let us remember the following especially important note taken from the experience of the ascetics all demonic manifestations are of such a nature that even minute attention to them is dangerous, for such attention [even if] allowed without any special sympathy to the manifestation, can make a most harmful impression, and result in a serious temptation.

Humility in reasoning is inseparable from spiritual reasoning. Saint Isaac the Syrian tells us that "only the one who has humility can be acknowledged as reasonable; the one who has not humility, will never achieve wise reasoning (Homily 28). A living faith reveals God to the eyes of the soul; the Word of God unites the soul with God. One who comes to see God in this way, who has felt God in this way, realises his unworthiness and is filled with unutterable reverence toward God, toward all His acts, toward all His ordinances, toward all His teaching, and gains humility in reasoning. The humble in reasoning will not be emboldened even to be curious about that which is performed outside the Will of God, that which has been condemned in proper time by the Word of God; the signs of the Antichrist will be alien to one humble in reasoning, since he has no relation to them. The recognition of one's own unworthiness and weakness, and the seeing of God, His majesty, power and eternal goodness, give rise in the soul to a striving with prayer to God. The hope of such a soul is concentrated on God, and that is why it is not distracted at prayer; the soul prays, uniting into one all its strength, and strives towards God with all its being. The soul resorts to prayer as often as possible, it prays unceasingly. At the arrival of the great sorrows at the time of the Antichrist, all who truly believe in God will cry out with a magnified prayer to God (Saint Ephraim the Syrian, Homily 106). They will cry out for help, for defence, for the sending of Divine Grace to strengthen them and to lead them. Their own strength, although they are faithful to God, is insufficient to stand against the united powers of fallen angels and men, who will act with rage and despair, sensing their own imminent destruction (Rev. 12:12).

Divine Grace, over-shadowing the elect of God, will make them immune to the wiles of the seducer and fearless before his threats, casting a disdainful eye on his miracles. Divine Grace will give the elect courage to confess the Saviour, Who has accomplished the salvation of mankind, and it will denounce the false messiah, who came to destroy mankind. It will lead the elect to places of execution as if to a royal throne, or a wedding feast. The experience of love for God is sweeter than the experience of life (A thought echoed by the holy martyr James the Persian. See his Life, November 26). As death and the suffering accompanying death comprise the beginning of eternal torment for a sinner, so the suffering for Christ and a martyric death for Him comprise the beginning of the eternal joys of paradise. This we see from the action of Divine Grace on the martyrs of the first centuries of Christianity. At first they were allowed to demonstrate their inclination; upon the acceptance of the first sufferings, help from on high came upon them, making their suffering and death for Christ most desirable. The Lord, prophesying the sorrows which must be before His Second Coming, commanded His disciples to watch and pray: *Take ye heed, watch and pray* (Mark 13:33). Prayer is always needful and beneficial for man; it keeps him in communion with God and under God's protection; it keeps him from self confidence, from seduction by vanity and pride, both from that which comes from his own fallen state, and from that arising in thoughts and dreams from the realm of the fallen spirits. In times of sorrows and dangers, seen and unseen, prayer is especially needful, being an expression of denial of self confidence, an expression of hope in God, drawing to us God's assistance. The All powerful God becomes the active agent for the one who prays in difficult circumstances, and He leads His servant out of them by His miraculous Providence.

Knowledge of God, living faith, blessed humility of mind, and pure prayer are attributes of spiritual reasoning, they are essential parts of it. On the contrary, ignorance of God, unbelief, blindness of spirit, pride, self confidence and self conceit are elements of a carnal mind. Such a mind does not know God, does not accept and does not understand the means offered by God for receiving knowledge of God, and thus creates for itself a mistaken, soul destructing means for the acquisition of the knowledge of God, in accordance with its own state it asks for a *sign from heaven.* Amen.

On the Deadening of the Human Spirit

A Sermon on the Sunday of the Myrrh-bearing Women

Today's Gospel passage proclaims the actions of the holy women who followed the God-man during His earthly sojourn, who were witnesses to His Passion and were present at His burial. The burial took place on Friday evening. When the malice of the Jews was being poured forth like fiery lava from fire-breathing Mount Etna, directed not only at the Lord but also at all those close to Him; when the holy Apostles were forced to hide themselves, or were only able to observe the terrible event from afar; when only the most intimate disciple of love, who was afraid of nothing, remained persistently by the Lord—then that disciple took action who had always been a disciple in secret, and who had continually concealed his heartfelt pledge out of fear of being persecuted by the Sanhedrin. Joseph—a respected member of the Sanhedrin—suddenly trampled down all the obstacles and vacillations and all the bewilderment that had hitherto constrained and worried him. He came to cold, cruel Pilate and asked for the body of Him Who had been executed by means of a shameful death. He received the body and buried it with reverence and honor. The Gospel imparts to Joseph's act the significance of a magnanimous, courageous action. And that is just what it was. A member of the Sanhedrin—before the face of the Sanhedrin, which had committed deicide; before the face of Jerusalem, which had taken part in the deicide—took the body of the God-man, Who had been murdered by men, down from the Cross and bore it away to a garden situated close to the city gates and walls. There—in solitude and quiet, under the shade of the trees, in a new tomb cut out of the solid rock face, with an abundant outpouring of fragrant spices and myrrh—he placed the body, by which the bodies and souls of all mankind have been redeemed, having wrapped it in the purest linens, the way a precious treasure is wrapped and concealed.

Another member of the Sanhedrin took part in the burial: Nicodemus, who had come to the Lord by night, and who had recognized Him as the One sent by God. Having leaned a great stone against the door of the sepulcher (in the Gospel the low opening into the cave is called a door), Joseph left, as one who had completed his service satisfactorily. The Sanhedrin was watching Joseph's actions. After his departure they took care to set a guard at the sepulcher and to affix a seal to the stone that blocked the entrance. The Lord's burial was witnessed by His persecutors and enemies. Some members of the Sanhedrin, having in a frenzy and rage committed the greatest crime, had involuntarily performed the greatest sacrificial offering: by sacrificing the all-holy Victim they had redeemed mankind and had put an end to the fruitless series of archetypal sacrifices, making those sacrifices and their statutes themselves superfluous. Other members of the Sanhedrin, representatives of all the righteous ones of the Old Testament, in a God-pleasing way and spirit performed the burial of the Redeemer of men, and by this action completed and sealed the pious work of the sons of the Old Testament. Henceforth commences the exclusive ministry of the figures of the New Testament.

The holy women were no less courageous than Joseph in their self-renunciation. Having been present at the burial on Friday, they did not consider it permissible on the Sabbath—the day of rest—to disturb the repose in which the Lord's body slept in the sacred darkness and reclusion of the cave-sepulcher. The women intended to pour out their zeal for the Lord by pouring myrrh on His body. Having returned from the burial on Friday, they straightway bought a sizable quantity of fragrant mixtures of spices and awaited the day following the Sabbath. On that day, at the rising of the sun, the pious women set out for the tomb. On the way they remembered that a large stone had been rolled in front of the tomb's entrance. This caused them to worry, and the women began to speak among themselves: *Who shall roll us away the stone from the door of the sepulcher?* (Mark 16:3). The stone was *very great.* When they arrived at the sepulcher, to their surprise they saw the stone rolled away. It had been moved aside by a resplendent, powerful angel. After the Lord's Resurrection the angel had descended from heaven to the tomb that had held Him Whom the heavens could not contain. He had struck the guards with fear, and at the same time had broken the seal and moved the heavy stone aside. He was sitting upon the stone, awaiting the arrival of the women. When they came he proclaimed to them the Lord's Resurrection, commanding them to inform the Apostles. Thanks to their zeal towards the God-man, thanks to their resolution to render honor to the all-holy body—guarded by sentries and vigilantly watched by the hatred of the Sanhedrin—the holy women were the first people to receive precise and reliable information about Christ's Resurrection. They became the first and most powerful preachers of the Resurrection, since they had heard the news from the mouth of an angel. There is no partiality with the all-perfect God: all are equal before Him, and that man who strives toward God with great self-renunciation is made worthy of the special gifts of God, in exceptional abundance and with spiritual beauty.

Who shall roll us away the stone from the door of the sepulcher? These words of the holy women have a mystical meaning. It is so edifying that love for my neighbor and desire for his spiritual benefit do not permit me to be silent about it.

The tomb is our heart. Our heart was a temple, but it has become a tomb. Christ enters therein by means of the sacrament of Baptism, in order to dwell within us and act through us. Then the heart is consecrated to God as a temple. We take from Christ the possibility of acting, and we revive our "old man," when we continually act according to the inclination of our fallen will and of our reason, poisoned by falsehood. Christ, Who entered at Baptism, continues to abide in us, but He is as it were wounded and put to death by our behavior. The temple of God, not made with hands, is turned into a cramped and dark tomb. A stone, *very great,* is rolled against the entrance. The enemies of God set a watch before the tomb, and with a seal they make fast the opening that is shut up by the stone. They seal the stone to the rock wall so that, in addition to the weight, the substantial seal might prohibit one from touching the stone. The enemies of God themselves keep watch to preserve this deadening! They have deliberated and have set up every kind of obstacle to warn them in advance of a resurrection—to prevent it, to make it impossible.

The stone is that infirmity of the soul by which all other infirmities are kept inviolable, and which the Holy Fathers call "insensibility."[1] What is this sin? Many will say that they have never even heard of it. According to the definition of the Fathers, "insensibility" is the deadening of spiritual feelings. It is the invisible death of the human soul regarding spiritual matters and a total revitalization regarding material matters.

It happens that due to a long-term physical illness, all one's strength is exhausted and all the body's faculties wither. Then the sickness, not finding food for itself, ceases to torment the bodily frame. It leaves the sick one worn out—deadened, as it were—and incapable of activity because he has been wasted by sufferings, because of a terrible, mute sickness which is not expressed by any particular kind of suffering. The same thing happens in a human soul as well. A long-standing negligent life amidst continual distractions, amidst continual voluntary sins, in forgetfulness of God and eternity, in forgetfulness of—or in the most superficial remembrance of—the Gospel commandments and teachings, removes one's feeling for spiritual matters and deadens the soul to them.

---

[1] See St. John Climacus, *The Ladder of Divine Ascent,* Step 18.

Though these spiritual matters exist, they cease to exist for him, because his life has ceased for them—all his strength is directed only to that which is material, temporal, empty, and sinful.

Anyone who examines the state of his soul dispassionately and thoroughly will see in it the infirmity of insensibility. He will see the extent of its influence, he will see its severity and importance, and he will admit that it is the manifestation and evidence of the deadening of his soul. When we want to take up the reading of the word of God, what boredom attacks us! Everything we read seems to be of little importance, undeserving of attention, strange! How we wish to be quickly freed from this reading! To what is this due? It is due to the fact that we have no feeling for the word of God.

When we stand at prayer, what dryness and coldness we feel! How we rush to finish our superficial supplications, filled with distractions! Why is this? Because we are strangers to God: we believe in the existence of God with a dead faith. He does not exist for our feelings. Why have we forgotten eternity? Is it possible that we will be excluded from the number of those who must enter its boundless domain? Is it possible that death does not stand before us face-to-face as it stands before other men? What is the reason for this? It is because we have become attached with all our soul to material things. We never think about eternity, and we never want to think about it—we have lost our precious presentiment of it and have acquired a false concern for our earthly sojourn. This false feeling makes our earthly life seem to us to be endless. We are so deceived and captivated by this false feeling that we arrange all of our actions in accordance with it. We offer up the faculties of our soul and body in sacrifice to that which is corruptible, taking no care at all for the other world which awaits us, even though we must without fail become eternal inhabitants of that world. Why do idle talk, joking, judgment of our neighbors, and biting mockery of them pour forth from us as from a spring? Why is it that without feeling burdened we spend many hours at the most shallow entertainments without finding satiety in them, and endeavor to replace one empty occupation with another, while we do not want to dedicate even the briefest time to the examination of our sins and to weeping over them? It is because we have acquired a feeling for sin, for everything shallow, for everything through which sin is introduced into man, and by which sin is preserved in man. It is because we have lost the feeling for everything that introduces the God-beloved virtues into man, and increases and preserves them in him.

Insensibility is inculcated in a soul by the world which is hostile toward God and by the fallen angels who are hostile toward God, and with the cooperation of our own will. It grows and is strengthened by a life that conforms to the principles of the world. It grows and is strengthened by following one's own fallen reason and will, ceasing to serve God, and serving God negligently. When insensibility tarries in one's soul and becomes its nature, then the world and the rulers of the world affix their seal to the stone. This seal consists in the human spirit's contact with the fallen spirits, in the human spirit's assimilation of the impressions produced on it by them, and in its subjugation to the forcible influence and predominance of the rejected spirits. *Who shall roll us away the stone from the door of the sepulcher?* This is a question filled with anxiety, sadness, and bewilderment. This anxiety, sadness, and bewilderment are felt by those souls who are making their way to the Lord, having ceased serving the world and sin. Before their gaze is revealed, in all its terrible magnitude and significance, the infirmity of insensibility. They desire to pray with contrition, to read the word of God without desiring to read other things, and to abide in continual contemplation of their sinfulness, in continual pain over it. In a word, they want to be adopted by God, to belong to God, and they encounter something unexpected—an opposition within themselves that is not comprehended by the servants of the world: insensibility of heart. Their heart, struck by their previous negligent life as if by a mortal wound, displays no signs of life. In vain does their mind gather thoughts about death, about God's Judgment, about the multitude of their sins, about the torments of hell and the delights of paradise. In vain does their mind try to smite their heart with these thoughts—it remains without feeling for them, as if hell, paradise, God's Judgment, one's own transgression, and one's state of fallenness and perdition had no relation whatsoever to the heart. It sleeps a deep sleep, a sleep of death. It sleeps, drunk and intoxicated with sinful poison. *Who shall roll us away the stone from the door of the sepulcher?* This stone is *very great.*

According to the teachings of the Holy Fathers, in order to destroy insensibility man needs a constant, patient, uninterrupted activity against insensibility; he needs a constant, pious, and attentive life. The life of insensibility is put to shame by such a life. But this death of the human spirit is not put to death by man's efforts alone: insensibility is destroyed by the action of Divine Grace. An angel of God, at God's command, comes down to the aid of a toiling and troubled soul, rolls away the stone of hardness from his heart, fills his soul with contrition, and proclaims to the soul its resurrection, which is the usual result of constant contrition.[2] Contrition is the first sign of the quickening of the heart with regard to God and eternity. What is contrition? Contrition is a man's feeling of mercy and compassion for himself—for his disastrous state, his state of fallenness, his state of eternal death. Concerning the people of Jerusalem who were brought to this frame of mind by the preaching of the holy Apostle Peter and became disposed to accept Christianity, the Scripture says that *they were pricked in their heart* (Acts 2:37).[3]

The Lord's body had no need of the fragrant myrrh of the myrrh-bearers. The anointing with myrrh was forestalled by the Resurrection. But the holy women—by their timely purchase of myrrh, by their early walk to the life-bearing tomb at the sun's first rays, by their disregard of the fear that had been instilled in them by the malice of the Sanhedrin and the military watch that stood guard over the tomb and the One buried therein—manifested and proved by their actions their heartfelt care for the Lord. Their gift turned out to be superfluous, but it was recompensed a hundredfold by the appearance of the angel, who had hitherto been invisible to the women, and by the news—which could not fail to be utterly true—of the Resurrection of the God-man, and the resurrection with Him of all mankind. God does not need for Himself the dedication of our lives, the dedication of all our strength and capabilities to His service—but for us it is indispensable. We offer them as myrrh at the Lord's tomb. Let us opportunely buy myrrh as an offering of love. From our youth let us renounce all sacrifices to sin. At the price of this renunciation let us buy myrrh, as an offering of love. Service to sin cannot be combined with service to God: the first destroys the second. Let us not permit sin to mortify the feeling for God and for all things Divine in our spirit! Let us not allow sin to place its seal upon us, to receive a violent predominance over us.

He who has entered into the service of God from the days of his unspoiled youth, and who remains in this service with constancy, submits himself to the continual influence of the Holy Spirit. He is imprinted with the Grace-filled, all-holy impressions which proceed from Him, and he acquires, in time, an active knowledge of Christ's Resurrection. In Christ he comes to life in spirit and is made, by the election and command of

---

[2] See St. John Climacus, *The Ladder of Divine Ascent*, 1:6.
[3] In the Slavonic Scripture it is said that they became contrite in heart.–*Trans.*

God, a preacher of the Resurrection to his brethren. He who through ignorance or fascination has enslaved himself to sin, has entered into a relationship with the fallen spirits, has numbered himself among them, and has lost within his spirit his bond with God and with the inhabitants of heaven—let him be healed through repentance. Let us not put off our treatment from one day to the next, that death may not steal upon us unexpectedly; that it may not carry us off suddenly; that we may not turn out to be incapable of entering into the habitations of unending repose and festivity; that we may not be cast, like useless tares, into the fire of hell, which forever burns and is never quenched. Chronic diseases are not quickly cured, and not as easily as ignorance imagines. It is not without reason that God's mercy grants us time for repentance; it is not without reason that all the saints implored God that they be granted time for repentance. Time is needed for the blotting out of sinful impressions; time is needed to be imprinted with the stamp of the Holy Spirit; time is needed to cleanse ourselves from impurity; time is needed to be clothed in the raiment of the virtues, to be adorned with the God-loving qualities with which all the inhabitants of heaven are adorned.

Christ is resurrected in a man who is prepared for it, and the tomb—the heart—again becomes a temple of God. *Arise O Lord, save me, O my God* (Ps. 3:7). In this, Thy mystical and, at the same time, substantial Resurrection, consists my salvation. Amen.

On Vigilance[4]

Let the fear of God outweigh all other sensations upon the scales of your heart; and then will it be convenient to for you to be vigilant toward yourself, both in the silence of your kellia [cell] and in the midst of the noise that surrounds you from all sides.

A well-reasoned moderation in foodstuffs, diminishing the passionate heat of his blood, tends greatly to facilitate your being able to attend to yourself; while the impassioning of your blood, stemming, as it does, from an excessive consumption of foodstuffs, from extreme and intensified bodily movements, from the inflammation of wrath, from being heady with vanity, and by reason of other causes, gives rise to a multitude of thoughts and reveries—in other words, to distraction. The Holy Fathers, first of all, ascribe to such a one as is desirous of attending to himself a moderate, evenly-measured, constant abstention from food.[5]

Upon awakening from sleep—an image of the awakening from the dead, which awaits all men—direct your thoughts to God, offering up to Him the first-thoughts of your mind, which has not yet become imprinted with any vain impressions whatsoever.

Having carefully fulfilled all the needs of the flesh upon arising from sleep, quietly read your customary rule of prayer, taking care not so much for the quantity of your prayerful expression, as for the quality of it; i.e., do it attentively, so that, by reason of your attention, your heart might be enlightened and enlivened through prayerful feeling and consolation. Upon concluding your rule of prayer, do you again, direct all your strength to the attentive reading of the New Testament, primarily the Evangel. In the course of this reading, intently take note of all the instructions and commandments of Christ, so that you might direct all your actions—both manifest and veiled—in accordance with them.

The quantity of the reading is determined by one's strength and by one's circumstances. It is unnecessary to weight-down one's mind with an excessive reading of prayers and Scripture; likewise, is it unnecessary to neglect one's needs in order to practice immoderate prayer and reading. Just as the excessive use of foodstuffs disorders and weakens the belly, so too does the immoderate use of spiritual food weaken the mind and create in it a revulsion to pious practices, leading it to despair.[6]

---

[4] Written for a Certain Layman As a Result of His Desire To Live A Vigilant Life In The World by St. Ignatius Brianchaninov

[5] (Dobrotoliubiye [Philokalia], Pt. II, Ch. of St. Filofei [Philotheus] of the Sinai)

For the novice, the Holy Fathers suggest frequent—but brief—prayers. When one's mind matures with spiritual age, becoming stronger and more manly, then shall one be in proper condition to pray without ceasing. It is to such Christians as have attained to maturity in the Lord that the words of the Apostle Paul pertain:

"I desire, therefore, that men pray everywhere, lifting up holy hands, without anger and reproach." (I Tim. II, 8) i.e., dispassionately, and without any distraction or inconstancy. For that which is natural to the man is not yet natural to the infant.

Enlightened, through prayer and reading, by our Lord, Jesus Christ, the Sun of Righteousness, one may then go forth to carry out the affairs of one's daily course, vigilantly taking care that in all one's deeds and words, in one's entire being, the All-holy will of God might prevail, as it was revealed and explained to men in the Commandments of the Evangel.

Should there be any free moments during the course of the day, use them to read attentively some chosen prayers, or some chosen portions of Scripture; and, by means of these, fortify the powers of your soul, which have become exhausted through activity in the midst of a world of vanities.

Should there not be any such golden moments, it is necessary to regret their loss, as though it were the loss of a valuable treasure. What is wasted today should not be lost on the day following, because our heart conveniently gives itself up to negligence and forgetfulness, which lead to that dismal ignorance, so ruinous of Divine activity, of the activity of man's salvation.

Should you chance to say or to do something that is contrary to God's commandments, immediately treat your fault with repentance; and, by means of sincere contrition, return to the Way of God, from which you stepped aside through your violation of God's will. Do not linger outside the Way of God! Respond with faith and humility to sinful thoughts, reveries and sensations by opposing to them the Gospel commandments, and saying, along with the holy patriarch Joseph:

"How shall I speak this evil word and sin before God?" (Gen. XXX, 9)

One who is vigilant toward oneself must refuse himself all reverie, in general—regardless of how attractive and well-appearing it might seem,

---

[6] ([St.] Isaak the Syrian, "Sermon 71")

for all reverie is the wandering of the mind, which flatters and deceives it, while being outside the truth, in the land of non-existent phantoms, and incapable of realization. The consequences of reverie are: loss of vigilance toward oneself, dissipation of the mind, and hardness of heart during prayer, whence comes distress of the soul.

In the evening, departing into slumber—which, in relation to the day just past, is death—examine your actions during the course of that day. Such [self-] examination is not difficult, since, in leading an attentive attentive life, that forgetfulness which is so natural to a distracted man is destroyed through vigilance toward oneself. And so, having recollected all your sins, whether through act, or word, or thought, or sensation, offer your repentance to God for them, with both the disposition and the heart-felt pledge of self-amendment. Later, having read the rule of prayer, conclude the day which was begun by meditating upon God by meditating, once again, upon God. Whither do they depart—all the thoughts and feelings of a sleeping man? What mysterious state of being is this sleep, during which the soul and body are both alive and yet not alive, being alienated from the awareness of their life, as though dead? Sleep is as incomprehensible as death. In the course of it, one's soul reposes, forgetting the most-cruel earthly afflictions and calamities that have beset it, while it images its eternal repose; while one's body (!!) ... if it rises from sleep will also arise, inevitably, from the dead.

The great Agafon said: "It is impossible to succeed in virtue without exerting vigilance toward oneself."[7]

Amen.

---

[7] (The Patericon of Skete)

On Reading The Gospels[8]

When reading the Gospel, do not seek pleasure, do not seek exalted states, and do not seek brilliant thoughts—seek to see the unadulterated, holy truth.

Do not be satisfied with a mere fruitless reading of the Gospel; strive to fulfill its commandments, and read it with your deeds. This is the book of life, and you have to read it with your life.

Do not think that there is no reason why the most sacred of books, the Four Gospels, begins with the Gospel of St. Matthew and ends with the Gospel of St. John. Matthew teaches more about how to fulfill God's will, and his instructions are particularly appropriate for beginners on the path to God; John expounds upon the image of the union of God with man renewed by the commandments, which is something accessible only to those who are progressing along the divine path.

When opening the book of the Holy Gospel to read it, remember that it decides your fate. We will be judged according to it, and depending upon how we were here on Earth with regard to it, we will receive our lot either in eternal blessedness, or eternal punishment (cf. Jn. 12:48).

God revealed His will to a paltry speck of dust: man! In your hands is the book in which His great and all-holy will has been set forth. You can accept it, or you can reject the will of your Creator and Savior—it all depends upon what you yourself want. Your eternal life and eternal death are in your own hands—just think how careful and wise you must be. Do not trifle with your eternal fate!

Pray with a contrite spirit to the Lord, so that He would open your eyes to see the wonders hidden in His Law (cf. Ps. 118:18), which is the Gospel. Your eyes will be opened, and you will behold the wondrous healing of the soul from sin, which is wrought by God's word. The very healing of bodily infirmities was merely proof of the healing of the soul—proof for fleshly people, for minds palsied by sensuality (cf. Lk. 5:24).

Read the Gospels with extreme reverence and attention. Do not consider anything in them to be of little importance or unworthy of full contemplation. Every iota of it radiates life. And to be negligible about life is death.

Read about the lepers, the paralyzed, the blind, the lame, and the demonically possessed whom the Lord healed; contemplate the fact that your soul, which bears many different forms of the wounds of sin

---

[8] From *Ascetical Experience* by St. Ignatius (Brianchaninov)

and is held captive by the demons, is just like these sick people. Learn from the Gospel to have faith that the Lord Who healed them will also heal you, if you will diligently pray to Him for your healing.

Acquire a disposition of soul that enables you to receive healing. Those who are capable of receiving healing are those who recognize their sinfulness and resolve to abandon it (cf. Jn 9:39-41). For the proud righteous man, that is, the sinner, who does not see his sinfulness, the Savior is unnecessary and useless (cf. Matt. 9:13).

Vision of our sins, vision of the fallen state that the entire human race is in, is a special gift of God. Pray down this gift for yourself, and the Heavenly Doctor's book—the Gospels—will be more comprehensible to you.

Strive to assimilate the Gospel with your mind and heart, so that your mind would, so to speak, swim in it, live in it. Then your activities will more readily become evangelical. This can be achieved through constant, reverent reading and study of the Bible.

St. Pachomius the Great, one of the most well known of the ancient fathers, knew the Holy Gospel by heart and imputed to his disciples, as God revealed to him, the essential need to learn it. In this way the Gospel accompanied them everywhere, and guided them always.

Even now, why shouldn't Christian educators adorn the memories of innocent children with the Gospel, instead of littering them with Aesop's fables and various sorts of rubbish?

What happiness, what riches is the acquisition of the Gospels by memory! We can't foresee the drastic changes and catastrophes that can happen to us throughout our earthly life. When it is possessed by memory the Gospel can be read by the blind; it goes to prison with the prisoner; it speaks to the laborer in the field, bedewing him; it instructs the judge during the trial; it guides the merchant at the market; it gladdens the sick during exhausting sleeplessness and oppressive solitude.

Do not dare to explain the Gospel and other books of Holy Scripture yourself. The Scriptures were pronounced by the holy prophets and apostles, and they were pronounced not at their own will, but by the inspiration of the Holy Spirit (cf. 2 Pet. 1:21). How could it be anything but madness to explain them according to our own will?

Having pronounced the word of God through the prophets and apostles, the Holy Spirit expounded upon it through the holy fathers. And both the word of God and its explanation are gifts of the Holy Spirit. This is the only explanation the Holy Orthodox Church accepts! This is the only explanation accepted by her true children!

Whoever explains the Gospels and all the Scriptures according to his own will thus rejects the explanation of them by the holy fathers, the Holy Spirit. Whoever rejects the explanation of Scripture by the Holy Spirit, undoubtedly rejects also the Holy Scriptures themselves.

And it can happen that the word of God, the word of salvation, for its presumptuous exegists becomes the savour of death, a double-edged sword, with which they pierce themselves unto eternal perdition (cf. 2 Pet 3:16; 2 Cor 2:15–16). <u>Arius</u>, Nestorius, Eutichius, and other heretics murdered themselves forever with it, for they willfully and presumptuously explained the Scriptures unto blasphemy.

But to this man will I look, even to him that is poor and of a contrite spirit, and trembleth at my word (Is. 66:2) says the Lord. Be this way with regard to the Gospels and the Lord, Who is present in them.

Leave your sinful life behind, leave your earthly passions and pleasures, renounce them with your soul, and then the Gospel will become accessible and understandable to you.

The Lord says, *He that hateth his life in this world*—the soul who has rejected fallennness and love of sin as if by nature, as if by his life—*shall keep it* [his life] *unto life eternal* (Jn. 12:25). But the Gospel is closed to him who loves his own life, who does not have the resolve for self-denial; he reads the letters, but the word of life as the Spirit remains hidden from him as if behind an impenetrable veil. When the Lord was on earth in His most pure flesh, many saw Him, while many others did not. What good is it when a person looks with his bodily eyes, which he possesses in common with the animals, but sees nothing with the eyes of his soul—the mind and heart? And these days as well, many read the Gospel and yet have never read it, and do not know it at all.

As one venerable desert dweller said, the Gospel must be read with a pure mind, and is understood according to the measure that the reader fulfills its commandments by his deeds. But it is not possible to acquire a precise and perfect revelation of the Gospel through your own efforts—this is a gift of Christ.

When the Holy Spirit has come to abide in the His true and faithful servant, He makes him also a perfect reader, and a true fulfiller of the Gospel.

The Gospel is a depiction of the qualities of the new Man, Who is *The Lord from Heaven* (1 Cor. 15:47). This new Man is God by nature. The holy tribe of His people, who believe in Him and are transformed in Him, He makes gods according to grace.

You who are wallowing in the stinking, filthy morass of sins and find pleasure in this! Lift up your heads and look at the pure heavens—that is your place! God gives you the dignity of gods, and you, rejecting that dignity, choose another worth for yourself: the worth of animals—and the most impure ones at that. Come to your senses! Leave that foul-smelling morass, cleanse yourselves with the confession of your sins, wash yourselves with tears of repentance, make yourselves beautiful with tears of contrition, rise from the earth and ascend to the heavens—the Gospel summons you there. *While ye have light*—The Gospel, in which Christ is hidden as a treasure—*believe in the light, that ye may be the children of Light*—which is Christ (Jn 12:36).

On Reading the Holy Fathers[9]

Conversation and association with one's neighbors very much affects a person. Conversation and acquaintance with a learned man communicates much knowledge; with a poet, many exalted thoughts and feelings; with a traveler, much information about countries, about the characters and customs of peoples. It is obvious that conversation and acquaintance with the saints communicates holiness. "With the holy man wilt thou be holy, and with the innocent man wilt thou be innocent. And with the elect man wilt thou be elect" (Psalms 17:25-26).

From henceforth, during the time of this short earthly life, which Scripture has not even called "life," but rather "journeying," let us become acquainted with the saints. Do you want to belong to their society in heaven, do you want to be a partaker of their blessedness? From henceforth enter into association with them. When you go forth from the house of the body, then they will receive you to themselves as their own acquaintance, as their own friend (Luke 16:9).

There is no closer acquaintance, there is no tighter bond, than the bond of oneness of thoughts, oneness of feelings, oneness of goal (I Corinthians 1:10).

Where there is oneness of thoughts, there without fail is oneness of soul, there without fail is one goal, an identical success in the attaining of one's goal.

Appropriate to yourself the thoughts and the spirit of the Holy Fathers by reading their writings. The Holy Fathers attained the goal: salvation. And you will attain this goal by the natural course of things. As one who is of one thought and one soul with the Holy Fathers, you will be saved.

Heaven received into its blessed bosom the Holy Fathers. By this it has borne witness that the thoughts, feelings, and actions of the Holy Fathers are well-pleasing to it. The Holy Fathers set forth their thoughts, their heart, the image of their activity in their writings. This means: what a true guidance to heaven, which is borne witness to by heaven itself, are the writings of the Fathers.

The writings of the Holy Fathers are all composed by the inspiration or under the influence of the Holy Spirit. Wondrous is the agreement among them, wondrous is the anointing! One who is guided by them has without any doubt whatsoever the guidance of the Holy Spirit.

---

[9] From *Living Orthodoxy* (Vol. XVII, No. 2, March-April 1995)

All the waters of the earth flow together into the ocean, and it may be that the ocean serves as the beginning of all the waters of the earth. The writings of the fathers are all united in the Gospel; they all incline towards teaching us the exact fulfillment of the commandments of our Lord Jesus Christ; of all of them both the source and the end is the holy Gospel.

The Holy Fathers teach how to approach the Gospel, how to read it, how to understand it correctly, what helps and what hinders in comprehending it. And therefore in the beginning occupy yourself with the reading of the Fathers. When they have taught you how to read the Gospel, then read the Gospel primarily.

Do not consider it sufficient for yourself to read the Gospel alone, without the reading of the Holy Fathers! This is a proud, dangerous thought. Better, let the Holy Fathers lead you to the Gospel, as their beloved child who has received his preparatory upbringing and education by means of their writings.

Many people, all who have senselessly and presumptuously rejected the Holy Fathers, who have come without any intermediary, with a blind audacity, with an impure mind and heart to the Gospel, have fallen into fatal delusion. The Gospel has rejected them; it grants access to itself only to the humble.

The reading of the Fathers' writings is the father and the king of all virtues. From the reading of the Fathers' writings we learn the true understanding of Holy Scripture, right faith, the way of life in accord with the Gospel's commandments, the deep esteem which one should have toward the Gospel commandments—to say it in a word, one learns salvation and Christian perfection.

Because of the diminishing of Spirit-bearing instructors, the reading of the Fathers' writings has become the main guide for those who wish to be saved and even attain Christian perfection. (*Rule of St. Nil Sorsky*)

The books of the Holy Fathers, as one of them has expressed it, are like a mirror; looking into them attentively and frequently, a soul can see all of its shortcomings.

Again, these books are like a rich collection of medicinal means; in them the soul can seek for each of its illnesses a saving remedy.

St. Ephphanius of Cyprus said, "A mere glance at holy books arouses one towards the pious life." (*Alphabetic Patericon*)

The reading of the Holy Fathers should be careful, attentive, and constant; our invisible enemy, who hates the voice of confirmation (Proverbs 11:15), hates especially when this voice comes forth from the

Holy Fathers. This voice unmasks the wiles of our enemy, his evilness, reveals his snares, his way of working; and therefore the enemy arms himself against the reading of the Fathers by various proud and blasphemous thoughts, tries to cause the ascetic to fall into vain cares in order to distract him from this saving reading, fights with him by means of despondency, depression, forgetfulness. From this warfare against the reading of the Holy Fathers we should conclude how saving (is) the weaponry for us, by the degree to which it is hated by the enemy. The enemy makes all efforts to wrest it out of our hands.

Let each personally choose for himself the reading from the Fathers which corresponds to his way of life. Let the hermit read the Fathers who wrote about the solitary life; let the monk who lives in the cenobitic life read the Fathers who wrote instructions for cenobitic monks; let the Christian who lives in the world read the Holy Fathers who pronounced their teachings for all Christianity in general. Let everyone, in whatsoever calling he be, draw forth abundant instruction in the writings of the Fathers.

It is absolutely necessary that the reading correspond to one's way of life. Otherwise you will be filled with thoughts which, although holy, will be unfulfillable in the actual deed and will arouse you to fruitless activity in only the imagination and desire; the work of piety which does correspond to your way of life will slip out of your hands. Not only will you become a fruitless dreamer—your thoughts, being in constant opposition to your sphere of activity, will without fail give birth to turmoil in your heart, and to uncertainty in your conduct, which are burdensome and harmful for you and for your neighbors. By an incorrect reading of Holy Scripture and the Holy Fathers, one can easily deviate from the saving path into impassable thickets and deep abysses, which has happened with many. Amen.

The Activity of Prayer Is the Highest Activity of the Human Mind

The one who seeks corruptible earthly blessings in his prayer rouses the indignation of Heaven's King against himself. The angels and archangels-His courtiers-behold you during your prayer, they see what you are requesting from God. They are surprised and rejoice when they see an earthly creature leave the earth behind and make a request to receive something heavenly, but they mourn for the one who ignores the heavenly and asks for earth and decay.

We are commanded to be children in malice, but not in understanding (1 Corinthians 14:20).

During prayer, the reason of this world, which is verbose and conceited, is cast off; this does not mean that feeblemindedness is applied or required. Perfected reason is required, spiritual reason, filled with humility and simplicity, which is often expressed in prayer not through words, but by prayerful silence which surpasses words. Prayerful silence then envelops the mind, when suddenly new, spiritual understanding appears to it which is inexpressible in the words of this world and age, when an especially vivid feeling of God being present arises. Before the inscrutable greatness of the Divine Being, His feeble creature, man, falls silent.

Vain repetitions (Matthew 6, 7-8), condemned by the Lord in the prayers of pagans, consist in multiple requests for temporal blessings, which fill the prayers of pagans, as well as the eloquent manner in which they are made, as if rhetorical flourishes, material sonority and the power of the word can act on God in the same way that they act on the hearing and nerves of people of flesh. In condemning this verbosity the Lord did not at all condemn prolonged prayers, as it seemed to some heretics: for He Himself blessed prolonged prayer by being in prayer at length. And continued all night in prayer to God (Luke 6:12) as the Gospel recounts of the Lord.

The lengthiness of the prayers of God's saints is not due to verbosity, but to their abundant spiritual feelings, which are manifest in them during prayer. Time, so to speak, is destroyed by the abundance and strength of these feelings, hence it is transformed into eternity for the saints of God.

When the one who prays achieves attainment in his holy podvig, then the variety of thoughts in the psalms and other words of prayer does not correspond to his disposition. The prayer of the tax collector and other very brief prayers give a more satisfactory expression of the inexpressible, expansive desire of the heart and God's saints have often spent many hours, days and years in such prayer without feeling any need of variety of thoughts for their powerful, concentrated prayer.

Prayers composed by heretics are immensely similar to the prayers of pagans: there is verbosity in them, the earthly beauty of the word, the inflaming of the blood, a lack of repentance, striving for the wedding-feast of the Son of God from the pagan temple of the passions itself and delusion. They are alien to the Holy Spirit-the deadly infection of the dark spirit wafts from them- the spirit of the evil one, the spirit of lies and destruction.

How great the activity of prayer is! The holy apostles refused to serve their neighbours in their fleshly needs, in order to pray and to serve the word. It is not reason, they said, that we should leave the word of God and serve tables… We will…give ourselves to prayer, and to the ministry of the word, (Acts 6:2-4) meaning in conversation with God through prayer and in conversation about God with their neighbours, proclaiming the Triune God and the Word of God made man to them.

The activity of prayer is the highest activity of the human mind; the state of purity, estranged from distraction, which is granted to the mind by prayer, is its highest natural state; the mind's rapture in God, of which the primary cause is pure prayer, is a supernatural state.

Only the holy saints of God arise to this supernatural state who, having been renewed by the Holy Spirit, having taken off the old Adam and been clothed in the New and able with the open face of the soul to behold the glory of the Lord, are being transformed into the same image…from glory to glory by the action of the Spirit of the Lord. (2 Corinthians 3:18). They receive most of their Divine revelations during the exercise of prayer, as this is a time when the soul is especially prepared, especially purified and inclined to communication with God. Thus, the holy apostle Peter saw a special sheet descending from heaven during prayer (Acts 10:11). Thus, an angel appeared to Cornelius the Centurion during prayer (Acts 10: 3). Thus, the apostle Paul was praying in the temple at Jerusalem when the Lord appeared to him and ordered him to leave Jerusalem immediately. Depart, for I will send thee far hence unto the Gentiles, He said to him (Acts 22 17:21).

Learn to Pray to God in the Right Way

As it is natural for the destitute to beg, it is natural for man, who has been reduced to poverty by the fall, to pray.

Prayer is fallen and repentant man turning towards God. Prayer is the weeping of fallen and repentant man before God. Prayer is fallen man, slain by sin, pouring out the desires, supplications and laments of his heart before God.

The first revelation, the first movement of repentance is the weeping of the heart. This is the heart's voice of prayer, which comes before the prayer of the mind. For soon the mind, taken up by the prayer of the heart, begins to produce prayerful thoughts.

God is the sole source of all true blessings. Prayer is the mother and the chief of all the virtues, as it is both the means and state of man's communion with God. It derives virtues from the source of blessings, from God, and assimilates them to man when he tries to be in communion with God.

The way to God is prayer. The measure of the way undertaken is the various prayerful states, into which the one who prays gradually enters, constantly and in the right way.

Learn to pray to God in the right way. Having learned how to pray in the right way, pray constantly and you will duly inherit salvation. Salvation comes from God in its own time, as it irrefutably reveals itself in the heart to the one who prays constantly and in the right way.

For prayer to be right, it must be brought forth from a heart filled with poverty of spirit, a heart which is broken and contrite. B before it is renewed by the Holy Spirit, all the other states of the heart- for you have to admit that this is exactly what they are-are not fitting for the repentant sinner who entreats God to forgive his sins and to free him from enslavement to the passions, as from a dungeon and chains.

By the law of Moses, the Israelites were directed that only one place had been appointed by God for them to offer up all their sacrifices. And by the spiritual law, one spiritual place is appointed for Christians to offer up all of their sacrifices but most particularly the sacrifice of sacrifices- prayer. This place is humility.

God does not need our prayers! He knows what we need before we ask Him; He, the Most Merciful, pours out lavish generosities on those who do not ask Him. It is we who need prayer: it assimilates man to God. Without it, man is estranged from God, yet the more he practices prayer, the more he comes close to God.

Prayer is the Eucharist of life. Neglecting it brings the soul unseen death.

The Holy Spirit is, to the life of the soul, what air is to the life of the body. The soul breathes this holy, mysterious air by means of prayer.

When you rise from sleep, let your first thought be of God; offer up to God the very beginning of your thoughts which have not yet been marked by any vain impressions. When you are falling asleep, when you are preparing to sink into that image of death, let your last thoughts be of eternity and God reigning therein.

An angel revealed to a certain holy monk the following pattern of thoughts in prayer, which is well-pleasing to God: the beginning of prayer must be composed of the glorifying of God, of thanksgiving to God for His innumerable blessings; then we must offer up to God a sincere confession of our sins in contrition of spirit; to conclude we can put forward, but with great humility, requests to the Lord for the needs of our soul and body, reverently leaving the fulfilment or non-fulfilment of these requests to His will.

The initial basis of prayer is faith: *I believed, therefore I have spoken* (Psalm 116:10) through my prayer to merciful God, Who has graciously commanded me to pray and vowed to heed it.

Therefore I say unto you, what things soever ye desire, when ye pray, believe that ye receive them and ye shall have them (Mark 11:24), proclaimed the Lord. So therefore, casting aside any doubt or doublemindedness, be persistent in prayer before the Lord, who commanded us *always to pray and not to faint*; (Luke 18:1) that is not to fall into despondency from the constriction of prayer, which, especially at the beginning, is burdensome, unbearable for a mind which has grown used to wandering. Blessed is the soul, which constantly knocks at the door of God's mercy through prayer and through complaints about its *adversary* (Luke 18:3) -about the sin which oppresses it- constantly *wearying the Unwearying One:* in time this soul will rejoice in its purity and dispassion. Sometimes our request is heard immediately; but sometimes, in the words of the Saviour, God *bears long with us* (Luke 18:7), that is to say he fulfils what we have asked slowly: He sees that delaying this fulfilment for a time is necessary for our humility; that we need to languish; to see our powerlessness, which is always discovered abruptly when we are left to ourselves.

Prayer, like a conversation with God, is a great blessing in itself; often to a much greater extent than the things that man requests,-and merciful

God leaves the supplicant in prayer through not fulfilling their request, in order that he does not forego it and does not abandon this higher blessing when he receives the one he asked for, which was a far lesser blessing.

God does not meet requests if the fulfilment of them is bound together with harmful consequences; He doesn't meet those requests which are contrary to His holy will, contrary to His wise, unfathomable destinies.

The great Moses, the God-seer, made a request contrary to God's purpose, that it would be granted to him to enter the promised land and he was not heard (Deuteronomy 3:26); holy David prayed, strengthening prayer with fasting, ashes and tears, for the life of his son who had fallen ill to be saved, but he was not heard (2 Samuel 12). And you, when your request is not fulfilled by God, yield reverently to the will of the All-Holy God, Who for unfathomable reasons has left your request unfulfilled.

To the children of the world, who ask God for earthly blessings to satisfy earthly lusts, the holy apostle James preaches: *Ye ask and ye receive not, because ye ask amiss, that ye may consume it upon your lusts* (James 4:3).

When we wish to have an audience with an earthly king, we prepare for this with particular care: we examine what the disposition of our heart might be when conversing with him so that we will not be distracted by the outburst of some emotion into a phrase or a gesture which will not please him; we envisage beforehand what we will say to him so that we only say what is proper and thereby make him disposed to us; we take care so that our outward appearance attracts his attention. We should make the proper preparation all the more when we wish to come before the King of kings and enter into conversation with Him through prayer.

Man looketh on the outward appearance, but the Lord looketh on the heart (1 Samuel 16:7); but in man, the disposition of the heart corresponds in particular to the expression of his face, his outward appearance. So therefore have the most reverential pose during prayer. Stand like a condemned man hanging his head, not daring to look up at the sky, with his hands at his sides or holding them behind as if they were tied together with rope, in the way that criminals are usually tied up when they have been seized at the scene of the crime. Let the sound of your voice be the pitiful sound of weeping, the groan of someone who has been wounded by a lethal weapon or suffering a harrowing illness.

God looketh on the heart. He sees our most hidden, most subtle thoughts and feelings; he sees all our past and all our future. God is everywhere present. So therefore stand in your prayer as if you were standing before God Himself. For you are indeed standing before Him! You are standing before your Judge and almighty Lord, on Whom depends your lot in time and eternity. Use your audience with Him to establish your wellbeing; do not let this audience, through your unworthiness, serve for you as grounds for temporal and eternal punishments.

Do Not Seek Enjoyment in Prayer

The soul of prayer is attention. Just as the body is dead without the soul, prayer without attention is dead. The spoken prayer turns into empty words without attention and the one who prays is counted amongst those who *take the Lord's name in vain*.

Pronounce the words of the prayer unhurriedly; do not allow the mind to wander about but enclose it in the words of the prayer. This path is narrow and sorrowful for a mind which is used to drifting freely about the world, this path leads to attention. Whoever tastes the great blessing of attention will love to constrict the mind on the path which leads to holy attention.

Attention is the initial gift of divine grace which is sent down to the one who labours and patiently endures in the *podvig* (ascetic struggle) of prayer.

One's own efforts towards attention should precede the attention bestowed by God-the former should be the active evidence of a sincere desire to receive the latter. One's own attention is gripped by thoughts and dreams and is shaken by them; attention bestowed by God is steadfast.

Renounce distraction of thoughts in prayer, despise daydreaming, dispel cares by the power of faith, strike fear of God into your heart and duly you will become habituated to attention.

The praying mind must be in a completely sincere state. A dream, however fetching and enticing it may be, is the frivolous creation of one's own mind and takes the mind out of the state of divine truth and leads it into a state of self-delusion and deception, hence it is cast aside in prayer.

During prayer, your mind should be free of images and you should thus preserve it carefully, dispelling all images which spring up through the power of the imagination, for the mind in prayer stands before God who is unseen, Who cannot be represented in any material way. If the mind allows images in prayer, they become an impenetrable curtain, a wall between the mind and God. "Those who see nothing in their prayers, see God," said venerable Meletius the Confessor.

If the image of Christ appears to you during your prayer either tangibly or makes itself manifest in your mind, or the image of an angel or any saint-in short, whatever image it is, do not take this appearance for a real one at all and pay no attention to it whatsoever, do not enter into conversation with it. Otherwise, you will be certain to become subject to delusion and to the most powerful spiritual injury, as has happened to many people. Man is incapable of communing with holy spirits until he is renewed by the Holy Spirit. As he still finds himself in the realm of fallen spirits, in their captivity and under their enslavement, he is only capable of seeing them and they often appear to him, having noted high self-regard and delusion within him, in the guise of angels of light or in the guise of Christ Himself to destroy his soul.

The holy Church uses holy icons to stir up devout remembrances and feelings and not at all to stir up daydreaming. When you stand before the icon of the Saviour, stand as if you were before the Lord Jesus Christ Himself, who is everywhere present in His divinity as well as present in His icon; when you stand before the icon of the Mother of God, stand as if you were before the Most-Holy Virgin Herself- but keep your mind free of images: there is the greatest difference between being in the presence of Lord, standing before the Lord and visualizing the Lord. The feeling of the Lord's presence brings a salutary fear over the soul, imbues it with a salutary feeling of reverence, but visualizing the Lord and His saints imparts a sort of materiality to the mind and leads it into false, proud self-regard and leads the soul into a false state, the state of delusion.

The feeling of God's presence is such a high state! It is by this that the mind is kept from conversing with extraneous thoughts which vilify prayer; it is by this that man's nothingness is strongly felt and that a special vigilance over oneself is made manifest, preserving man from even the slightest sins. The feeling of God's presence is attained by attentive prayer. Reverently standing before holy icons greatly enables one to obtain this.

The words of the prayer, enlivened by attention, penetrate deep into the soul, wound and pierce, so to speak, the heart and imbue it with tenderness. The words of a prayer said in distraction seem only to touch the surface of the soul, making no impression on it at all.

Attention and tenderness of heart are recognised as the gift of the Holy Spirit. Only the Spirit can make the rushing waves of the mind cease, said Saint John Climacus. Another venerable father said "When we have tenderness of heart, then God is with us", (Hieromonk Seraphim of Sarov).

The one who has attained constant attention and tenderness of heart in his prayers has attained the state of those blessings which are called *poverty of spirit and mourning* in the Gospel. He has already broken many of the chains of the passions and has already scented the aroma of spiritual freedom, he already bears the foundation of salvation in his core. Do not abandon the constrictions of true prayer and you will obtain holy peace, the mysterious sabbath: for no earthly tasks are done on the sabbath, the battle and *podvig* recede; in holy dispassion, without distraction, the soul stands before God in pure prayer and is at peace in Him through faith in His eternal goodness and by devotion to His all-holy will.

Attainment in prayer is first made manifest in the one who is an ascetic of prayer through the particular action of attention: it unexpectedly envelops the mind from time to time, encloses it in the words of the prayer. Then attention becomes far more constant and lengthier: the mind seems to latch onto the words of the prayer and is carried off by them towards union with the heart. Finally, tenderness of heart is suddenly added to attention, making man into a temple of prayer, into God's temple.

Offer up to God prayers which are quiet and humble and not passionate or fiery. When you become the mysterious priest of prayer, you will go up into God's tabernacle and from there you will fill the censer of prayer with holy fire. It is forbidden to offer up to All-Holy God the unclean fire-the blind and material inflaming of the blood.

The holy fire of prayer which is bestowed from God's tabernacle is holy love, poured out upon true Christians by the Holy Spirit (Romans 5:5). The one who strives to combine prayer with the fire of the blood imagines, in his delusion, deceived by his self-regard, that he does service to God, when he actually rouses His anger.

Do not seek enjoyment in prayer: this is not at all natural for the sinner. The desire of the sinner to feel enjoyment is indeed delusion. Seek for your dead and hardened heart to come alive, so that it is opened up to feel its own sinfulness, its fall and unworthiness, so that it can see them and admit them with self-abandonment. Then the true fruit of prayer will be found in you-true repentance. You will groan before God and cry out to Him through prayer from the wretched state of the soul which has suddenly revealed itself to you; you will cry out as if from a dungeon, from the grave, from hell.

Repentance produces prayer and this daughter produces it two-fold.

Enjoyment in prayer is only the lot of the holy saints of God, who have been renewed by the Holy Spirit. The one who is distracted by the impulses of the blood, distracted by vainglory and sensuality and fabricates his own enjoyment, is in woeful delusion. The soul which is darkened by living according to the flesh, the soul deceived and deceiving itself by its pride is very capable of such fabrications.

The feelings produced by prayer and repentance are a lightening of the conscience in the world of the soul, reconciliation with one's neighbour and the circumstances of life, mercy and compassion for humanity, refraining from the passions, coldness towards the world, obedience to God, strength in the struggle against sinful thoughts and distractions. Be content with these feelings, which do contain the savour of the hope of salvation. Don't seek high spiritual states and delights in prayer prematurely. They are actually not at all as they appear to our imagination: the action of the Holy Spirit, from Whom the high states of prayer come, is inscrutable for the mind of flesh.

Learn to pray with all your mind, with all your soul and with all your strength. You might ask: what does this mean? You cannot find out in any other way than through experience. Try to constantly be occupied with attentive prayer: attentive prayer will grant you the answer to this question through holy experience.

The *podvig* of prayer appears onerous, boring and dry to a mind which is habituated to only being occupied with corruptible objects. The ability to pray is obtained with difficulty; when this ability is obtained then it becomes the source of constant spiritual consolation.

Prayer, as has been said above, is the mother of the virtues- obtain this mother, then! Her children will proceed from thence into the house of your soul and will make it into God's shrine.

Offer up prayer to God before you begin any undertaking; draw God's blessing onto your undertakings through this and judge your actions by this: the thought of prayer causes us to refrain from actions which are against God's commandments.

The one who turns to God in prayer before any word or action, for instruction, assistance and blessing, carries out his way of life as if under God's gaze and under His guidance. This ability is beneficial; nothing is swifter than the mind, said Barsanuphius the Great, nothing is more beneficial than to raise the mind to God when you encounter any need. (Answer 216).

In the difficult circumstances of life, offer your prayers to God more frequently. It is better to resort to prayers than to the empty notions of weak human reason which mostly cannot come to pass. It is better to lean on faith and on the almighty God through prayer than on one's feeble reason through untrustworthy notions and assumptions.

Do not be mindless in your requests, so as not to anger God by your thoughtlessness: the one who asks for something negligible from the King of Heaven thus dishonours Him. The Israelites, when they had ignored God's miracles enacted for them in the desert, asked for fulfilment of the desires of the belly, *but while their meat was yet in their mouths, the wrath of God came upon them* (Psalm 78:30-31).

Offer up to God requests which measure up to His greatness. Solomon asked Him for wisdom and received it, as well as many other blessings, because he asked wisely. Elisha asked Him for the two-fold grace of the Holy Spirit, before his great teacher, and his request was accepted.

On Spiritual Deception

Thy mind was deluded: it tasted the fruit forbidden by God. The fruit seemed to be beautiful with a curious, careless glance at it; the fruit seemed to be beautiful for the ignorance, inexperience, innocence; the malicious and sly counsel persuaded the eating of it; the eating of the fruit struck the one who ate with the death. The bitterness of the poisonous eatable still foaming at thy mouth; thy inside is tormented of acting of poison in it. Confusion, bewilderment, clouding, disbelief comprehend thy soul. Exhausted, frustrated by sin, you look back, being before directed to the kingdom of God ... (Luke VI, 62. Lam. 1.)

Disciple: Give an accurate and detailed concept of spiritual deception.[10] What exactly is this condition?

Elder: Spiritual deception is the wounding of human nature by falsehood. Spiritual deception is the state of all men without exception, and it has been made possible by the fall of our original parents. All of us are subject to spiritual deception. Awareness of this fact is the greatest protection against it. Likewise, the greatest spiritual deception of all is to consider oneself free from it. We are all deceived, all deluded; we all find ourselves in a condition of falsehood; we all need to be liberated by the Truth. The Truth is our Lord Jesus Christ (Jn. 8:32-14:6). Let us assimilate that Truth by faith in it; let us cry out in prayer to this Truth, and it will draw us out of the abyss of demonic deception and self-delusion. Bitter is our state! It is that prison from which we beseech that our souls be led out, that we may confess the name of the Lord (Ps. 141:8). It is that gloomy land into which our life has been cast by the enemy that hates and pursues us. It is that *carnal-mindedness* (Rom. 8:6) and *knowledge falsely so called* (I Tim. 6:20) wherewith the entire world is infected, refusing to acknowledge its illness, insisting, rather, that it is in the bloom of health. It is that "flesh and blood" which "*cannot inherit the Kingdom of God*" (I Cor. 15:50). It is that eternal death which is healed and destroyed by the Lord Jesus, Who is "*the Resurrection and the Life*" (Jn. 11:25). Such is our state. And the perception thereof is a new reason to weep. With tears let us cry out to the Lord Jesus to bring us out of prison, to draw us forth from the depths of the earth, and to wrest us from the jaws of death! "*For*

---

[10] [*prelest, delusion, illusion, spiritual delusion, spiritual deception* – all these English words in the article mean the same].

this cause did our Lord Jesus Christ descend to us," says the venerable Symeon the New Theologian, *"because he wanted to rescue us from captivity and from most wicked spiritual deception."*

Disciple: I do not sufficiently comprehend your explanation. I need a simpler explanation, more in keeping with my understanding.

Elder: The means whereby the fallen angel brought ruin upon the human race was falsehood (Gen. 3:13). For this reason did the Lord call the devil *"a liar, and the father of [lies]... a murderer from the beginning"* (Jn. 8:44). We see that the Lord closely associated the notion of falsehood with the notion of murder; for the latter is the inevitable consequence of the former. The words "from the beginning" indicate that from the very start the devil has used falsehood as a weapon in murdering men, for the ruination of men.

The beginning of evil is in the false thought. The source of self-delusion and demonic deception is the false thought. By means of falsehood, the devil infected mankind at its very root, our first parents, with eternal death. For our first parents were deceived, i.e., they acknowledged falsehood as the truth, and having accepted falsehood in the guise of truth, they wounded themselves incurably with mortal sin, as is attested by our ancestor Eve, when she said: *"The serpent deceived me, and I ate"* (Gen. 3:13). Thenceforth, our nature, infected with the poison of evil, has, voluntarily or involuntarily, inclined toward evil which, to our perverted will, distorted reason, and debauched heart, presents itself as good. I say voluntarily because there still remains within us a remnant of the freedom to choose between good and evil. And I say involuntarily because that remnant of freedom does not function as complete freedom, but rather under the unavoidable influence of the wound of sin. Thus is every human born and cannot be otherwise; and for this reason we all, without exception find ourselves in a state of self-delusion and demonic deception. From this view of man's state with regard to good and evil, the state which is necessarily characteristic of each human being, we arrive at the following definition of spiritual deception which explains it satisfactorily: **spiritual deception is man's assimilation of a falsehood which he accepts as truth**. Spiritual deception first acts upon one's way of thinking; on being accepted and having perverted one's thought processes, it is forthwith communicated to the heart whose sensibilities it distorts; having mastered the essence of man's being, it seeps into every one of his activities and poisons the very body which the Creator has indissolubly joined to the soul. The state of spiritual deception is the state of perdition or eternal death.

From the time of man's fall, the devil has had free access to him. The devil is entitled to this access, for, through obedience to him man has voluntarily submitted to his authority and rejected obedience to God. However, God has redeemed man. To the redeemed man He has given the freedom to submit either to God or to the devil; and that this freedom may manifest itself without any compulsion, the devil has been permitted access to man. It is quite natural that the devil makes every effort to keep man in his former subjection to him, or yet to enslave him even more thoroughly. To achieve this, he implements his primordial and customary weapon — falsehood. He strives to deceive and delude us, counting on our state of self-delusion. He stimulates our passions, our sick inclinations. He invests their pernicious demands with an attractive appearance and strives to entice us to indulge them. However, he that is faithful to the Word of God will not permit himself to do so; he will restrain the passions and thus repulse the enemy's assaults (see Jas. 4:7); struggling against his own self-deception under the guidance of the Gospel, subduing his passions, and thus gradually destroying the influence of the fallen spirits on himself, he will by stages pass from the state of deception to the realm of truth and freedom (see Jn 8:32), the fullness of which will be given through the overshadowing of divine grace. He that is not faithful to Christ's teaching, who follows his own will and knowledge, will submit to the enemy, and will pass from a state of self-deception into a state of demonic deception, will lose the remnant of his freedom, and in the end he will become totally enslaved to the devil. The state of those who are demonically deluded varies, depending upon the passion by which the particular individual is deluded and enslaved, and corresponding to the degree to which he is enslaved by that passion. And all those who have fallen into demonic delusion, i.e., those who, through the development of their own self-delusion, have entered into fellowship with the devil and have been enslaved by him, are temples and instruments of the demons, victims of eternal death, of life in the dungeons of hell.

Disciple: Enumerate for me the types of demonic delusion which result from the improper exercise of prayer.

Elder: All the forms of demonic delusion to which the athlete of prayer is subject arise from the fact that repentance has not been set as the foundation of prayer, that repentance has not been made the source, the soul, the goal of prayer. St. Gregory the Sinaite says: *"Should anyone fancy to attain unto exalted states of prayer with a self-confidence based on a conception of one's own worth, and has acquired not true zeal, but that of the devil, him wilt the devil easily enmesh in his snares as his slave."* Everyone who hastens to the wedding banquet of the Son of God, not in the clean and radiant garments wrought by repentance, but rather in the old rags of sinfulness and self-delusion, will be cast into the outermost darkness, into demonic deception. "I counsel thee," the Savior says to one whom He calls to the mystical priesthood, *"to buy of Me gold tried in the fire, that thou mayest be rich; and white raiment, that thou mayest be clothed, and that the shame of thy nakedness not appear; and to anoint thine eyes [of sense and the eyes of thy mind] with [the] salve [of tears], that thou mayest see. As many as I love, I rebuke and chasten; be zealous, therefore, and repent"* (Rev. 3:18-19). Repentance and everything that comprises it, such as: contrition or travail of spirit, lamentation of heart, tears, self-reproach, remembrance and foreboding of death, the judgment of God and the everlasting torments, the awareness of God's presence, fear of God — are all gifts of God, gifts of great worth, gifts which are basic and represent our assurance of loftier and eternal gifts. The latter you can never receive unless you have received the former. *"However great the life we may lead,"* says St. John of the Ladder, *"we may count it stale and spurious, if we have not acquired a contrite heart"* (Ladder of Divine Ascent, Step VII, 64). Repentance, contrition of spirit, and lamentation are signs which attest to the correctness of our feat of prayer. Their absence, on the other hand, is a sign of inclination towards false direction, self-delusion, deception and barrenness. One or the other, delusion or sterility, is the inevitable consequence of the incorrect exercise of prayer, and the incorrect exercise of prayer is inextricably bound up with self-deception.

The most dangerous and most incorrect method of prayer is when he who is praying fabricates, on the strength of his imagination, dreams or pictures, borrowing them ostensibly from the Sacred Scriptures, but in actuality from his own sinfulness and self-delusion. By means of those pictures he lures himself into self-esteem, vainglory, conceit and pride. It is apparent that all that is fabricated by the imagination of our fallen nature which has been perverted by the fall of nature does not exist in reality. It is nothing else but the fantasy and falsehood so characteristic and beloved of

Satan, the fallen angel. With the first step that he takes on the path of prayer, the fantast departs from the realm of truth and enters the realm of falsehood, the realm of Satan, and willingly submits to Satan's influence. St. Symeon the New Theologian describes the prayer of the fantast and its fruits thus: "He raises his arms, eyes, and mind toward heaven; and he fancies in his mind divine meetings, heavenly blessings, the ranks of the holy angels, the dwelling-places of the saints... in short, everything that he has heard of in the Divine Scriptures he gathers together in his imagination. He contemplates all that during his prayers and gazes heavenward, and spurring his soul on to divine desire and love, and sometimes he even sheds tears and weeps. His heart thus grows gradually bolder, without his oven being conscious of it. Not only that, but he also assumes that what is happening to him is the fruit of divine grace, conferred on him by the Lord for his consolation, and he entreats the Lord to vouchsafe him ever to abide in such spiritual activity. That is a sign of delusion. This sort of person cannot but fall subject to delirium and insanity, even though he observes perfect prayerful solitude. And even should he manage to avoid such a spiritual disaster, he nevertheless will never acquire a spiritual mind, virtue, or dispassion. In this manner those who have beheld light and radiance with their physical eyes, who savor sweet fragrances with their sense of smell, and hear voices with their ears, have been deceived. Some of them have become possessed by evil spirits and have wandered about, deranged, from place to place; others have accepted a demon that transformed himself into an angel of light, and were deceived and remained uncorrected even until the end of their lives, refusing the counsel of any of the brethren; still others, instructed by the devil, committed suicide; some cast themselves into an abyss, others hanged themselves. Who can enumerate the manifold deceptions of the devil which he uses to delude and which are inscrutable? Any knowledgable man can learn from what we have said as to the damage which ensues from this type of prayer. Such misfortunes befall mostly hermits who lead a solitary life, but it is possible that some of those who pray incorrectly will not fall subject to one of the calamities described above because they live in community with the brethren; yet such a person spends his whole life in vain.

All the holy Fathers who have described the struggle of mental prayer forbid not only arbitrary daydreams, but also assenting with our will and sympathy to dreams and apparitions that can unexpectedly present themselves to us regardless of our will. This happens during the exercise of prayer, particularly in the midst of stillness. *"Accept under no circumstances,"* says St. Gregory of Sinai, *"should you perceive anything either by your physical eyes or your mind, whether outside or within yourself, even should that be the visage of Christ, or of an angel, or of some saint, or should light appear to you. Be careful and cautious! Do not permit yourself to consent to anything, do not express sympathy or consent, do not hasten to trust an apparition, even should it turn out to be genuine and good. Better to remain cold and distant toward it, constantly preserving your mind devoid of images, free of any depictions and unmarked thereby. He that has perceived anything in thought or with the senses, even though it be from God, and who hastens to accept the apparition, easily falls into deception and ultimately discloses his inclination and capacity for it, because he accepts appearances readily and without discrimination. The beginner must direct all his attention to activity of the heart alone, and regard that alone as non-delusive. He should undertake nothing else until such time as he attains dispassion. God is not angry at one who, fearing deception, guards himself with extreme circumspection and thus does not accept some vision sent by God, without considering what was sent with all care. On the contrary, such a one will be praised by God for his clear thinking."* As an example, we may take the life of St. Amphilochius. He entered monasticism in his youth, and in his mature years and old age he was deemed worthy to lead the life of a hermit in the desert. Confining himself to a cave, he trained himself in stillness and was greatly successful therein. After forty years of solitary living, an angel appeared to him one night and said: "Amphilochius! Go thou to the city and shepherd the spiritual sheep!" Amphilochius, however, remained unperturbed and paid no heed to the angel's command. The following night, the angel again appeared and repeated his command, adding that it was sent by God. And once again Amphilochius did not submit to the angel, fearing lest he be deluded and mindful of the words of the Apostle, that Satan can appear even as an angel of light (II Cor. 11:14). But the angel returned once more on the third night, glorifying God in order thus to convince Amphilochius, for, as is generally known, the outcast spirits cannot bear this. Then the angel took the old man by the hand, led him out of his cell, and brought him to the church which stood nearby. The doors of the church opened of thorn selves. The church was illuminated with a heavenly light and a multitude of holy men in white robes were visible therein, their faces shining with a sun-like radiance. They consecrated Amphilochius as bishop of the city of Iconium. In contrast to this procedure, the venerable Isaac and Nicetas of the Kiev-Caves Lavra, while yet new and inexperienced in the solitary life, gullibly believed a vision which appeared to them and therefore fell into the most dreadful misfortune. To the former, a multitude of demons appeared in light; one of them assumed the guise of Christ, and the rest that of holy angels. The latter was first deceived by a demon by means of a sweet fragrance and voice, afterwards appearing to him openly in the guise of an angel. Monks who are experienced in the monastic life, truly holy monks, fear delusion far more, show a far greater distrust of themselves, than do beginners who are seized with fervent zeal for the ascetic struggle. The venerable Gregory of Sinai, the Hesychast, with heartfelt love warns us to guard ourselves against delusion. "*I desire,*" writes the saint in a book written chiefly for those who pray in solitude, "*that you have a clearly-defined understanding of delusion. I desire this with the goal in mind that you may be able to preserve yourself from delusion, that, in a struggle which has not been illumined by the necessary knowledge, you not inflict great damage upon yourself and destroy your soul. For man's free will readily inclines to fellowship with our adversaries, particularly the will of those who are inexperienced and new to the struggle, for they are still in the power of the demons.*" How true! Our free will does incline toward deception because every delusion flatters our self-esteem, our vainglory, our pride. "*The demons are close by and surround beginners and the arbitrary, spreading in their path the snares of evil thoughts and pernicious fantasies, digging for them abysses into which to plunge. The city of the novices,*" i.e., the entire being of each of them individually, "*is still under the suzerainty of the barbarians... Wherefore do not hasten to deliver yourself over to that which appears to you, but remain serious, holding on to what is good with much circumspection, and rejecting what is evil ... Know also that the effects of grace are always clear; the demon is incapable of producing them: he cannot give meekness or gentleness or humility or hatred of the world, and he does not restrain the passions of voluptuousness, as grace does. These are the effects of the devil: conceit, haughtiness, fear — in a word, all forms of malice. Therefore, by its activity will you be able to discern the light which shines in your soul, whether it be from God or from Satan.*" We ought to know, of course, that such circumspection is the property of advanced monks, never of beginners. The venerable Gregory of Sinai, it is true, is conversing with a beginner, but, as is evident from the book, a beginner in the life of prayerful stillness who was, according to the years he had spent in monasticism and from his age, already an elder.

Disciple: Did you have a chance to see someone who fell into the demonic delusion because of the development of dreaminess while practicing prayer?

Elder: Yes, I did. Some official, who lived in St. Petersburg, was practicing a severe feat of prayer, and it led him into an unusual state. He revealed to then archpriest of the Church of the Intercession of the Mother of God in Kolomna about his feat and its consequences. The archpriest, when visited some monastery in the Petersburg diocese, asked one of the monks of the monastery to talk with the official. "A strange state which the official has reached from the feat – fairly said the priest - may be more convenient to explain by the residents of a monastery, as they are more familiar with the details and cases of the ascetic feat." The monk agreed. After some time, the official arrived at the monastery. I witnessed his conversation with the monk. The official immediately began to speak about his visions – that he constantly saw the light from the icons during prayer, smelled fragrance, felt an extraordinary sweetness in the mouth, and so on. When the official finished the monk asked him, "Did it come to your mind, to kill yourself?" - "Of course!" - replied the official, "I was throwing myself (figure of speech used by the inhabitants of St. Petersburg) in the Fontanka river, but I was pulled out by others." It turned out that the official was using the type of prayer, described by Saint Symeon, which excited the imagination and blood, and making a man very capable of increased fasting and vigil. To the state of self-delusion, chosen randomly, the Devil has attached his own action, akin to that state – and the human self-delusion turned into an obvious prelest. The official saw the light with the bodily eyes: the fragrance and sweetness, which he felt, were also sensual. In contrast, the visions of saints and their supernatural states are quite spiritual (St. Isaac of Syria, Word 55): an ascetic becomes capable of them not before but after the eyes of the soul are opened by the Divine grace, in concurrence with this other feelings of the soul also come to life, hitherto being inactive (St. Symeon the New Theologian, the Word on Faith); the corporal senses of the saints also take part in the vision of grace, but only when the body will pass from the passionate state to the state of dispassion. The monk began to persuade the official to leave the employed method of prayer, explaining the incorrectness of both the method and the state, resulting from the method. The official resisted the advice fiercely: "How can I give up the obvious grace!" – he objected.

Listening attentively to what the official was telling about himself, I felt an inexplicable pity for him, and altogether he seemed to me somewhat funny. For example, he posed the following question to the monk: "When saliva increases in my mouth because of abundant sweetness, it starts to drip on the floor: is it a sin?" Exactly: people in the demonic delusion seem regrettable as not belonging to themselves, being with the mind and the heart prisoners of the evil, outcast spirit. They represent themselves a funny spectacle: they are made a laughing stock by the dominating sly spirit, who led them to a state of humiliation, having deceived by vainglory and arrogance. The deluded people do not understand either their captivity, or their strange behavior, no matter how obvious this captivity and strangeness of behavior is. - I was spending the winter of 1828-1829 at the Ploschanskaya Pustyn monastery (Orel diocese). At the time, an elder lived there, he was in prelest. He cut off his hand believing that he fulfilled a commandment from the Gospel, and he was telling anyone who was pleased to hear it, that the severed hand became a holy relic, that it was kept and honored in the Moscow Simonov monastery, that he, the elder, being at the Ploschanskaya Pustyn, five hundred miles from the Simonov monastery, felt when the Archimandrite of the Simonov monastery with the brethren venerated the hand. Sometimes a shudder passed through the elder and besides he started to hiss loudly: he recognized this phenomenon as a result of the prayer, but it seemed to be a perversion, worthy only of regret and laughter. Orphan children, who lived in the monastery, were amused by this phenomenon and copied it before the eyes of the elder. The elder came in anger, rushed at one and then at another boy and ruffled their hair. None of the venerable monks of the monastery could assure the deluded man that he is in the wrong state of mind, in a sickness of the soul.

When the official left, I asked the monk why he asked the official about the attempted suicide. The monk replied, "As minutes of unusual quiet of the conscience come during the mourning for God, which comprises the consolation of the mourners, contrary, the moments, when the delusion is revealed and allows to taste it as it is, come among the false pleasure from the devilish delusion. These minutes – are terrible! Their bitterness and the despair produced by this bitterness – are unbearable. This condition, which results from delusion, is an easy manifestation to notice the delusion for a deluded person and to take steps towards healing himself. Alas! The beginnig of prelest is pride, and the fruit of it is surpassing pride. The deluded man recognizes himself as a vessel of Divine grace, despises the saving warnings of the neighbours as it was seen by St. Symeon. Meanwhile, the fits of despair become stronger: finally, the despair turns into madness and is crowned by suicide. – Schemamonk Theodosius was living at the beginning of this [19th] century in the Sofronievaya Pustyn monastery (Kursk diocese). He gained the respect of both the brethren and the laity by a strict, higher living. Once it seemed to him that he was caught up into heaven. At the end of the vision, he went to the abbot, told in detail about the miracle, and he added an expression of regret that he had seen in heaven only himself and did not see any of the brethren. This trait slipped out of the spotlight of the abbot: he called the brethren, in contrite spirit told them about the vision of the schemamonk and admonished them to live a more diligent and God-pleasing life. After some time, some strangeness started to appear in the actions of the schemamonk. The matter ended with that he was found hanged himself in his cell".

The following case, worthy of noticing, happened to me. I was once visited by a schemamonk from Mt. Athos, who was in Russia for alms. We sat down in my own reception cell, and he started to speak to me, "Pray for me, Father, I sleep a lot and eat a lot." When he told me this, I felt the heat emanating from him, that is why I replied: "You do not eat a lot and do not sleep a lot; but is there anything peculiar in you?" and I asked him to enter my inner cell. Walking in front of him and opening the door into the inner cell, I prayed to God mentally, that He gave my hungry soul to borrow something from the hieroschemamonk from Athos if he – is a true servant of God. Exactly: I noticed something peculiar in him. In the inner cell, we again sat down for a talk, - and I started to ask him: "Do me a favor, teach me to pray. You live in the first monastic place on earth, among the thousands of monks: in such a place and in such a numerous gathering of monks, there should certainly be great ascetics of the prayer, knowing the mysterious action of the prayer and teaching this their neighbors, for example Gregory of Sinai and Palamas, following the example of many other Lights of Athos." The hieroschemamonk immediately agreed to be my mentor - and, horror of horrors! With the greatest excitement started he to teach me the above method of enthusiastic dreamy prayer. I saw he was in a terrible excitement! He got excited both the blood and the imagination! He was in self-satisfaction, delighted with himself, in self-delusion, in prelest! After he expressed himself, I began, in the rank of a disciple, to offer him the teachings of the Holy Fathers about prayer, pointing at them in the Philokalia, and asking him to explain this doctrine to me. The monk from Athos came in a perfect bewilderment. I saw he was quite unfamiliar with the teachings of the Fathers about prayer! As the conversation continued, I said to him: "Look, elder! If you live in St. Petersburg – do not take an apartment in the top floor, take an apartment certainly at the bottom." Why is that? – the monk from Athos objected. "Because, - I answered - if the angels suddenly want to take you, and move from St. Petersburg to Mount Athos, and if they carry you from the top floor but drop, you will be killed; if they carry you from the bottom floor and drop, you only will get a bruise." "Look – replied the monk - many times already when I was praying, I came to the actual thought that angels will take me and put on Mount Athos!" It turned out that the hieroschemamonk wore chains, hardly slept, ate little food and felt such a heat in the body that he didn't not need any warm clothes in winter. By the end of the conversation, it occurred to me to do the following: I started asking the monk, that as an ascetic and a faster, he tried himself the way of prayer taught by the Holy Fathers. The essence of this method is that during the prayer the mind is completely free from any dreams, and plunged into the attention to the words of the prayer, lay and be enclosed, according to St. John the Climacus, in the words of the prayer (The Ladder of Divine Ascent, Word 28, ch. 17). In this case, the heart usually helps the mind with the salutary feeling of sadness for sins, as St. Mark the Ascetic said: "*The mind, praying attentively, oppresses the heart: the heart of the contrite and humble God will not despise*" (Psal. 51; Word about those who have a false idea to be justified from the deeds, ch.34, Philokalia). "When you try it yourself, - I said to the monk - tell me about the fruit of the experience as well; for me, this experience is uncomfortable because of my relaxed life." The monk from Athos readily agreed to my proposal. In a few days, he came to me and said, "What have you done to me?" "Why are you asking?" - "When I tried to pray with attention, enclosing the mind in the words of prayer: all my visions disappeared, and now I no longer can get back to them." Later in a conversation with the monk, I did not see the arrogance and audacity which were very noticeable in him during the first meeting and which are commonly seen in people who are in self-delusion, who consider themselves to be holy or in a spiritual progress. The monk from Athos even expressed a desire to get my humble advice for himself. When I advised him not to differ from the other monks in the external way of life, because the distinction of oneself leads to arrogance (The Ladder of Divince Ascent, Word 4, Ch 2, 83; St. Barsanuphius the Great, answer 275; life and teachings of St. Apollos, Alphabet Patericon), he took off his chains and gave them to me. A month later, he visited me again, and said that the heat in his body ceased, he needed warm clothes and slept much more. In this respect, he said that on Mount Athos many people and even the ones, who have the fame of holiness, were using the way of prayer, which had been used by him – and taught it to the others. No wonder! St. Symeon the New Theologian, who lived eight centuries before our time, said that very few practise attentive prayer (About the third way of prayer). St. Gregory of Sinai, who lived in the fourteenth century after Christ, when arrived at Mount Athos, found that its numerous monks have no concept of noetic prayer and were engaged only in bodily feats, performing prayers only verbally and orally (Living of St. Gregory of Sinai). St. Nilus of Sora, who lived in the late 15th and early 16th century, also visited Mount Athos, said that in his time the number of people who practised attentive prayer minimized (Preface to the Tradition, or the Charter of the Skete). The elder, archimandrite Paisios Velichkovsky moved to Mount Athos from Moldova in 1747. He acquainted closely with all the monasteries and hermitages, talked to many of the elders, who were by the general opinion of the Holy Mountain recognized as experienced and holy monks. When he started to ask these monks about the books of the Holy Fathers who had written about noetic prayer it turned out that they neither knew about the existence of such writings, nor even knew the names of the Holy writers. By that time, Philokalia had not been yet printed in Greek (Excerpt from the letter of the elder Paisios to the elder Theodosius. Writings of Paisios, Optina Pustyn edition).

Attentive prayer requires self-sacrifice and very few dare self-sacrifice. The one who is enclosed in oneself with attention, being in a state of bewilderment from seeing their own sinfulness, unable to phrase-monger and in general to impress and act, appears somehow strange, mysterious, inadequate in all respects to the people who do not know this mystical feat. Is it not easy to give up the opinion of the world! And for the world – how to apprehend the true ascetic of prayer, when the very feat is even unknown to the world? What a difference – the one who is in self-delusion! He does not eat, does not drink, does not sleep, walks in winter with only a cassok on, wears chains, sees visions, teaches everyone and convicts with a bold impudence, without any regularity, senselessly and without meaning, with blood, carnal, passionate excitement, and because of this sad, fatal excitement. He is just a Holy one! The taste and desire for such people has long been noticed in the secular society: For ye suffer – writes the Apostle Paul to the Corinthians, if a man bring you into bondage, if a man devour you, if a man take of you, if a man exalt himself, if a man smite you on the face (2 Cor. 11,20). Then the holy Apostle says that he, being in Corinth, could not act boldly and brazenly: his behavior was caught with modesty, meekness and gentleness of the Christ (2 Cor.10, 1). Most of the ascetics of the Western Church proclaimed there as the greatest of saints – after its apostasy from the Eastern Church and after the retreat of the Holy Spirit from it – prayed using the above mentioned way and reached visions, of course, false. These imaginary saints were in a terrible demonic delusion. The delusion naturally arises on the basis of blasphemy that perverted the dogmatic faith for the heretics. The behavior of the Latin ascetics, filled with delusion, was always like frenzy, because of extraordinary corporal, passionate excitement. Ignatius of Loyola, the founder of the Order of Jesuits, was in this state. His imagination was so excited and sophisticated that, as he claimed, he could only wish and use some effort, and at his request either hell or heaven appeared before his eyes. The vision of heaven and hell were not produced solely by the action of human imagination; an act of human imagination alone is not enough for this: the vision was accomplished by the action of demons attaching their abundant action to insufficient human action, mating action with action, action to replenish the action on the basis of free will of a man, who chose and assimilated himself a wrong direction. It is known that the true saints of God are given visions only by the kindness of God and by the action of God, not by the will of a man and not by his own efforts – are given unexpectedly, very rarely, in the cases of special need, according to the wondrous providence of God, and not randomly (St. Isaac Syrian, Word 36). Enhanced feat of the ones, who are in prelest, usually adjoins deep depravity. Depravity is an assessment of that flame that inflames the deluded people. This is confirmed also by history and the testimony of the Fathers. "The one who sees the spirit of prelest – in the apparitions that it shows, - said St. Maximos Kavsokalivitis - is very often exposed to rage and anger; the incense of humility or prayer or a true tear has no place in him. On the contrary, he constantly boasts of his virtues, filled with vainglory, and devotes himself to sly passions fearlessly"(Conversation of St. Maximos with St. Gregory of Sinai).

Disciple: The incorrectness of this way of prayer and its relation to self-delusion and prelest – are clear; caution me also against other kinds of improper prayer and the false state connected to it.

Elder: As wrong action of the mind leads to self-delusion and prelest: exactly in the same way wrong action of the heart leads to it too. The desire and aspiration to see spiritual visions with the mind which was not purified from passions, not renewed and recreated by the right hand of the Holy Spirit, are filled with reckless pride: the same pride and recklessness fills the desire and aspiration of the heart to enjoy holy, spiritual and Divine sensations when the heart is unable to enjoy such pleasures. As the impure mind, wanting to see Divine visions and not being able to see them on its own, composes visions for itself and from itself, it is deceived and deluded by its own delusions: in the same way the heart, trying to taste the Divine sweetness and other Divine feelings and not finding them in itself, composes them from itself, using it to flatter itself, deluding, deceiving, destroying itself, entering the realm of falsehood, in communication with demons, submitting itself to their influence, enslaving itself by their power.

One sense out of all the sensations of the heart, in its state of fall, can be employed in the invisible Divine Service: sorrow for sins, about the sinfulness, the fall, the destruction. It is called weeping, repentance, and contrition of spirit. This is witnessed by the Holy Scripture. *For thou desirest not sacrifice; else would I give it: thou delightest not in burnt offering: both every feeling of the heart apart and all of them together are not pleasing to You, as contaminated by the sin, as perverted by the fall. The sacrifices of God are a broken spirit: a broken and a contrite heart, O God, thou wilt not despise.* (Ps. 51, 16-17). This sacrifice – a negative sacrifice, the offering of all other sacrifices with the offering of this sacrifice is naturally eliminated: if there is a feeling of repentance, all other sensations are silenced. For the sacrifices of other sensations to become pleasing to God, first the good pleasure of God must pour out in our Zion, first the walls of the destroyed Jerusalem must be built. Lord – is righteous, all-holy: only righteous, clean sacrifices, to which the human nature is capable after its renovation, are pleasing to righteous, all-holy God. He is not pleased with the desecrated sacrifices and burnt offerings. Let us take care to cleanse ourselves with repentance! Then shalt thou be pleased with the sacrifices of righteousness, with burnt offering and whole burnt offering: then shall they offer bullocks upon thine altar (Psal.51, 19): newborn feelings of a man, renewed by the Holy Spirit.

The first commandment given by the Savior to all of humanity without exception is the commandment about repentance: *From that time Jesus began to preach, and to say, Repent: for the kingdom of heaven is at hand.* (Matthew 4, 17). This commandment comprehends, includes combines all other commandments. The Savior said many times to those men who did not understand the value and power of repentance: *But go ye and learn what that meaneth, I will have mercy, and not sacrifice* (Matthew 9, 13). That means: the Lord in mercy for the fallen and lost men granted repentance to all as the only way to salvation, because all are seized with the fall and destruction. He does not charge, does not even want sacrifices from them, to which they are unable, but wishes that they would have mercy upon themselves, understand their disaster and free themselves from it by repentance. The Lord added to the noted words other fearful utterance: for I am not come, - He said - to call the righteous, but sinners to repentance. Who were called righteous? - Those miserable, blind sinners, who, being deceived by self-conceit, do not find repentance essentially necessary for themselves, and therefore, either reject it, or disregard it. Oh calamity! Because of that, the Savior denies them; they lose the treasure of salvation. "*Woe to the soul* - says St. Macarius the Great - *that does not feel its sores and thinks about itself, due to the great, infinite damage by the evil, that it is quite alien to the damage by the evil. Such souls are no longer visited and no longer cured by the good Doctor because it arbitrarily left its ulcers without care about them, and imagines about itself that it is healthy and immaculate. They that be whole need not a physician,* - he says, - *but they that are sick.*" (Matthew 9, 12; Word 6 on love, ch.16). A horrible cruelty to yourself – the rejection of repentance! A terrible coldness, lack of love for yourself - the neglect of repentance. The one, who is cruel to himself, cannot be not cruel for others as well. The one, who had mercy on himself by acceptance of repentance, together with that becomes a merciful and loving to the neighbors. This shows all importance of the error: take away from the heart something that was commanded to it by God Himself, a sense of repentance that is significantly and logically necessary for the heart. And make an effort to reveal in the heart, opposite to the order, in disregard of the establishment of God, those feelings, which should appear in the heart by themselves when it is cleansed by repentance, but in a very different character (St. Isaac of Syria, Word 55). A carnal man cannot have any notion of this spiritual character: because the notion of a felling is always based on the feelings that are already known to the heart, while spiritual feelings are quite alien to the heart, which knows only some carnal and emotional sensations. Such a heart does not know even about the existence of the spiritual experiences.

Everyone knows what a mental disaster came to the Jewish scribes and Pharisees because of their wrong disposition of the soul: they became not only alien to God, but His frantic enemies, killers of God. To such disasters are subjected those ascetics of prayer, who ejected repentance from their feat, striving to excite the love for God in the heart, striving to feel the pleasure, excitement: they develop their fall, make themselves aliens to God, come into communion with Satan, are infected with hatred for the Holy Spirit. This kind of prelest – is terrible: it is equally fatal for the soul as the first one, but is less evident; it rarely ends in madness, suicide, but definitely corrupts both the mind and the heart. Because of the state of mind that it produces, Fathers called it "conceit" (St. Gregory of Sinai, Word 108, 128; St. John of Karpathos, ch. 49). This kind of prelest is indicated by holy Apostle Paul when he says: *Let no man beguile you of your reward in a voluntary humility and worshipping of angels, intruding into those things which he hath not seen, vainly puffed up by his fleshly mind* (Col.2, 18). The one, who is obsessed with this kind of delusion, thinks about himself, creates an "opinion" about himself, that it has many virtues and merits – even that he has the abundance of the gifts of the Holy Spirit. This opinion is made up of false understanding and false feelings: within this its property, it quite belongs to the realm of the father and representative of falsehood – the Devil. The praying man, seeking to reveal in the heart the feelings of the new man and having no possibility for this, replaces them with the feelings of his own making, fake ones, which are immediately joined by the action of the fallen spirits. Upon recognizing the wrong feelings, own and demonic ones, as true and arising from grace, he acquires the ideas that correspond to these feelings. These feelings are constantly assimilated with the heart and, intensified in it, feed and multiply false ideas: it is natural that self-delusion and devilish prelest – "opinion", "conceit" – are formed from such wrong feat. "*A conceited opinion on something does not permit the subject to actually exist*" (Word 4, also at the end of Word 3), - said St. Symeon the New Theologian. The one who has a conceited opinion of himself that he is dispassionate, will never be cleansed from the passions; the one who imagines of himself that he is full of grace, will never receive grace; the one who thinks of himself that he is holy, will never reach holiness. Bluntly speaking: the one who attributes to himself any spiritual deeds, virtues, merits, gifts of grace, the one who flatters himself and entertains himself with "conceit", blocks with this "conceit" the entrance of the spiritual activity in himself, the entrance of the Christian virtues and Divine grace – he opens a wide entrance to the contagion of sin and demons. There is no longer capacity for spiritual progress in those who are infected with "conceit": they destroyed this ability, having brought to the altar of falsehood the very beginning of human activity and salvation – the notion of truth. An unusual pomposity is an attribute of the ones who are sick with this delusion: they seem to be intoxicated with themselves, with their state of self-delusion, seeing it as the state of grace. They are imbued, filled with arrogance and pride, though sounding humble for many, who judges by the face and who can not judge by the fruits, as the Savior has commanded (Matthew 7,16; 12,33), the less by the spiritual sense, which the Apostle refers to (Heb. 5, 14). The prophet Isaiah beautifully depicted the action of "conceit" in a fallen archangel, the action that deluded and killed the archangel. *For thou* - the prophet says to Satan - *hast said in thine heart, I will ascend into heaven, I will exalt my throne above the stars of God: I will sit also upon the mount of the congregation, in the sides of the north: I will ascend above the heights of the clouds; I will be like the most High. Yet thou shalt be brought down to hell, to the sides of the pit.* (Isaiah 14,13-15).

The Lord denounces the one who is infected with "conceit": *Because thou sayest, I am rich, and increased with goods, and have need of nothing; and knowest not that thou art wretched, and miserable, and poor, and blind, and naked* (Rev. 3,17). The Lord admonishes the deluded person to repent, offers to buy from nobody else but the Lord Himself the required needs, which constitute the repentance (Rev. 3:18). The purchase is strongly needed: there is no salvation without it. There is no salvation without repentance, and repentance is accepted from God only by those who, for accepting it, sell all their goods, that is, will renounce all that they falsely assimilated from "conceit".

Disciple: Did you meet anyone infected with this kind of prelest?

Elder: People infected with prelest of "conceit" are very common. Anyone who does not have a contrite spirit, who recognizes any own merits and achievements, anyone not holding steadily the teaching of the Orthodox Church, but discussing about any dogma or tradition arbitrarily, at his discretion, or according to the heterodox teaching, is in this kind of prelest. The degree of deviation and persistence of deviation determines the degree of prelest.

Feeble man! "Conceit" certainly creeps into us in some its form, and by executing of our "I", sends away from us the grace of God. As there is no, as noted by the St. Macarius the Great, person completely free from pride: there is no person who would be completely free from the action on him of a subtle delusion called "conceit". It was slandering Apostle Paul, and was healed by grievous allowances of God. *For we would not, brethren,* - writes the Apostle to the Corinthians - *have you ignorant of our trouble which came to us in Asia, that we were pressed out of measure, above strength, insomuch that we despaired even of life. But we had the sentence of death in ourselves, that we should not trust in ourselves, but in God which raiseth the dead* (2 Cor.1, 8-9). For this reason, we should vigilantly watch ourselves, so as not to attribute to ourselves any good deed, any praiseworthy virtue or special natural ability, even state of grace, if a person was raised into it, in short, not to recognize any dignity in oneself. *What hast thou,* - says the Apostle, - *that thou didst not receive* (1 Cor. 4.7) from God? From God we have both being and regeneration, and all the natural properties, all the abilities, both spiritual and bodily ones. We – are the debtors to God! Our debt is unpayable! From such a view on ourselves, the state opposite to "conceit" forms by itself for our spirit, the state that God called poverty of the spirit, which He commanded us to have and that He appeased (Matthew 5,3). The great tribulation – to deviate from the dogmatic and moral teachings of the Church, from the teaching of the Holy Spirit, by some kind of theorizing! This – *high thing that exalteth itself against the knowledge of God.* We should dethrone and captivate such knowledge into the *obedience of Christ* (2 Cor. 10, 4-5).

Disciple: Is there any connection between prelest of the first and the second kind?

Elder: The relationship between these two kinds of prelest certainly exists. Prelest of the first kind is always connected with prelest of the second kind, with "conceit". The one who composes seductive images by means of the natural ability of the imagination, constructing by means of dreaming (imagination) a charming picture from these images, the one who subordinates all his nature to the seductive, powerful influence of this painting, certainly, by the unfortunate necessity, thinks that the painting is made by the action of Divine grace, and that heart feelings that are excited by this painting, are sensations of grace.

The second kind of prelest – the "conceit" itself – acts without composing seductive pictures: it is content with composing fake feelings and states of grace, from which forms a false, perverse notion about the whole spiritual feat in general. The one, who is in the state of "conceit", acquires false outlook on everything around him. He is deceived both from inside and outside. Dreaminess acts strongly in the ones who are deluded with "conceit", but operates exclusively in the abstract field. It is either not involved at all, or rarely involved in painting of paradise, high palaces and mansions, heavenly light and fragrance, Christ, Angels and Saints in the imagination; it always composes apparently spiritual states, close fellowship with Jesus (Imitation of Thomas a Kempis, Book 2, Ch. 8), the internal conversation with Him (Book 3, Ch. 1), mystical revelations (Book 3, Ch. 3), voices, enjoyment; based on all this, it creates a false notion about oneself and about the Christian feat in general; creates a generally false way of thinking and disposition of the heart, leads either to the rapture at oneself or to the feverish and exaltation. These diverse feelings arise from the action of subtle vainglory and lust: from this action, the blood acquires a sinful, seductive movement that pretends to be a pleasure of grace. In turn, vainglory and lust are excited by the arrogance, this inseparable companion of "conceit". Terrible pride, like the pride of demons, is the dominant property of the ones who assimilated one or another prelest. Those who are deluded by prelest of the first kind, are lead by pride to the state of explicit madness; and in those who are in prelest of the second kind, it also produces damage to the mind that is called in the Scripture the *corruption of the mind* (2 Tim.3, 8), but is less noticeable, clothed in the guise of humility, piety, wisdom – is known by its bitter fruits. The ones who are infected with "opinion" about their own merits, especially about own holiness, are able and willing to do any torture, hypocrisy, cunning and deceit, all the atrocities. They breathe with implacable hostility against the ministers of truth, rush frantically at them when they do not recognize the state that it attributed to the deluded ones, that is exposed to the blind world by "conceit".

Disciple: Are there also spiritual states, produced by Divine grace, as the state in which a man tastes spiritual sweetness and joy, the state in which the secrets of Christianity are revealed, the state in which the presence of the Holy Spirit is felt in the heart, the state in which the devotee of Christ is awarded with spiritual visions?

Elder: Sure there are, but there are only in those Christians who have attained Christian perfection, pre-cleaned and prepared with repentance. Gradually, all action of repentance, which is expressed in all kinds of humility, especially the prayer that is brought out of the poverty of spirit, from weeping, progressively weakens the action of sin in man. This requires a lot of time. And it is given to true, loyal ascetics by the Providence of God, constantly keeping the watch over us. The struggle with the passions – is extremely useful: it most of all leads to poverty of spirit. With the aim of substantial benefit of our, the Judge and our God bears long with us, and does not soon avenge the opponent (Luk.18, 7) of our – the sin. When the passions weaken – it is done the most to the end of life (Living of Theophilus, Pimen the Much-ailing of the Kiev Caves, John The Much-suffering. Kiev Caves Patericon.) – then little by little, the spiritual states will begin to appear, distinguishing in everlasting difference from the states, composed by "conceit." Firstly, weeping that results from grace, enters the temple of the soul, washes and whitens it for the acceptance of gifts, subsequent to weeping according to the establishment of a spiritual law. The carnal man nowise, in no way can imagine the spiritual states, he can not have any concept of the weeping that is caused by grace: the knowledge of these conditions is acquired just by experience (St. Isaac of Syria, Word 55). Spiritual gifts are given by the Divine wisdom that watches that the verbal vessel, that must accept a gift, could endure the power of the gift without doing harm to itself. New wine perishes old bottles! (Matthew 9,17) It is noted that at present time, spiritual gifts are given with the greatest modesty, according to that weakness that fills almost all Christianity in general. These gifts meet the needs of almost only salvation. In contrast to that, the "conceit" gives its gifts in immeasurable abundance and with the greatest haste.

A common feature of the spiritual states – deep humility and humbleness of mind, coupled with a preference of all the neighbors to oneself, with the favor, evangelical love for all neighbors, with the desire to live in the obscurity, to break with the world. There is not enough space for "conceit" here: because humility is the renunciation of all own merits, in a substantial confession of the Redeemer, in recognition in Him of all hope and support, while "conceit" is to assign merits, given by God, to yourself, and in composing for ourselves non-existent merits. It is connected with the hope for oneself, with cold, superficial confession of the Redeemer. God is glorified to glorify Himself, as was glorified by the Pharisee (Luke 18,11). The ones who are obsessed with "conceit", for the most part are devoted to lust, despite the fact that they ascribe to themselves very exalted spiritual states, unprecedented in the correct Orthodox asceticism; a few of them refrain from a crude enslavement to lust – and refrain only because of the prevalence in them of the sin of the sins – pride.

Disciple: Is it possible for prelest that is called "conceit" to have any sensible visible miserable consequences?

Elder: Destructive heresies, schisms, atheism, blasphemy appeared from this kind of prelest. The unhappiest visible consequence of it is a wrong activity, pernicious for themselves and for others – evil, despite its clarity and breadth, little noticed and little understood. Unhappiness, evident for everyone, happens with the ones who practice prayer and who are infected with "conceit", but rarely because the "conceit", resulting in a terrible error of mind, does not lead the mind to frenzy as does the deranged imagination. – On the Valaam Island, in a distant desert hut, schemamonk Porphyrios lived, whom I saw myself. He was engaged in prayer feat.

What kind of feat was it – I absolutely do not know. One can guess the incorrectness of it from his favorite reading: the schemamonk thought highly about the book of the Western writer Thomas a Kempis, the Imitation of Jesus Christ, and was guided by it. This book was written from "conceit". One evening in autumn, Porphyrios visited the elders of the monastery, not far from which his hut was. When he said goodbye to the elders, they warned him, saying, "Do not you dare to go on the ice: the ice has just settled and is very thin." The hut of Porphyrios was separated from the monastery by a deep bay of Ladoga Lake, which had to be passed around. Schemamonk replied softly, with an outer modesty: "I have become light." He's gone. Through a short time they heard a desperate cry. The elders of the skete were alarmed, they ran out. It was dark; not soon they found the place where the accident had happened; not soon they found the means to get the drowned man: they dragged the body when it was already left by the soul.

Disciple: You are talking about the book "Imitation", which is written from a state of self-delusion, but it has a lot of readers, even among the children of the Orthodox Church!

Elder: These are those readers, delighted with its merits, who speak about these merits, not realizing that fact. In the preface to the book "Imitation" by a russian translator – 1834 edition, printed in Moscow – is said: "*One highly enlightened man – a Russian and Orthodox – used to say: if one were to ask my opinion, I would safely after the Holy Scripture put the book about imitation of Jesus Christ by Kempis*" (p.37). In this, such a decisive verdict, a heterodox writer is given preference to all the Holy Fathers of the Orthodox Church, and a person's own view is given preference before the definition of the whole Church, which at the holy Councils recognized the writings of the Holy Fathers to be Divinely inspired, and has left to read them, not only in edification of all the faithful, but also as a guidance in the Church matters. A great spiritual treasure is kept in the writings of the Fathers: the dogmatic moral tradition of the Holy Church. It is obvious that the book "Imitation" led the mentioned man in the mood from which he said so hastily, so wrong, so sad ("Imitation", at its original appearance, was condemned even by its own Latin Church, and persecuted by the Inquisition. Prosecution subsequently terminated, and reversed to the protection, when it was seen that the book is a good tool for propaganda among the people who have lost a true understanding of Christianity and kept a superficial approach to it. Under the name of papal propaganda is meant the spread of the concept of the Pope, which the Pope wants to suggest himself to humanity, i.e. the concept of the supreme, autocratic, absolute power of the Pope over the world. Propaganda, having this as an aim, pays little attention to the quality of teaching that it uses, everything suits it that contributes its aim – even the faith in Christ without leaving the faith in idols). This is – self-delusion! This is – prelest! It was composed from the false notions; false notions were born from the wrong sensations reported by the book. An anointing of the sly spirit lives and breathes from the book, who flatters the readers giving them a drink of falsehood, sweetened with the subtle flavorings of arrogance, vainglory and lust. The book leads readers directly to the communion with God, without pre-purification by repentance: that is why it excites a special sympathy among the passionate people who are not familiar with the way of repentance, not protected themselves from self-delusion and prelest, not instructed by the correct living by the teachings of the Holy Fathers of the Orthodox Church. The book makes a strong effect on the blood and nerves, excites them, – and that is why it is especially liked by the people enslaved by sensuality: you can enjoy this book without giving up the pleasures of rough sensuality. Arrogance, vainglory and subtle sensuality are proposed by the book as an action of God's grace. Having smelled their fornication in its own subtle action, carnal people come to the ecstasy of delights, of excitement delivered without labor, without self-denial, without repentance, without *crucifixion of the flesh with the affections and lusts* (Gal. 5:24), with the flattering of the sate of the fall. They gladly move, led by their blindness and pride, from the bed of bestial love to the bed of more felonious love that is dominant in the brothel of the outcast spirits. Some person, by the position of earth belonging to the highest and the most educated society, and on the exterior, to the Orthodox Church, expressed the following about a deceased Lutheran woman who was recognized by this person as holy, "*she passionately loved God, she thought only of God, and she had only seen God; she had only read the Gospel and "Imitation", which is the second Gospel*" (Ecstatic sentence was pronounced in French, so capable for the scene:"elle aimait Dieu avec passion; elle ne pensait qu'a Dieu, elle ne voyait que Dieu: elle ne lisait que l'Evangile qui est un second Evengile"). These words exactly express the state to which the readers and admirers of the "Imitation" are lead – This phrase is identical, in its essence, with the words of the famous French writer, Ms. de-Sevigne about the famous French poet, Racine older. "*He loves God* - allowed herself to say Ms. Sevine - *in the same way as he previously loved his concubines*"("Il aime Dieu, comme il aimait ses maitresses"). Known critic La Garp, a former atheist, who came to Christianity that he understood wrong and that he perverted, favoring the words of Ms. Sevigne said: "*The heart that loves the Creator and the creature – is one, although the effects vary among themselves as much how many the subjects are different*" ("C'est avec le meme coeur, qu'on aime ie Createur, ou la creature, quoique les effest soient aussi differente, quo les objets"). Racine moved from the debauchery to the delusion called "conceit". This prelest is expressed with all clarity in the last two tragedies of the poet: in "Esther" and "Athaliah". High Christian thoughts and feelings of Racine found a wide place in the temple of the Muses and Apollo (Apollo and the Muses – are the deity of the ancient pagans, Greeks and Romans, Pagans attributed the patronage of elegant Arts to these demons), in the theater – filed a delighted applause. "Athaliah", recognized as the supreme work of Racine, was staged forty-two times in a row. The spirit of this tragedy – is the one with the spirit of "Imitation".

We believe that there is a bestial desire in the human heart, the desire that was brought by the fall and that has a relationship with the desire of the fallen spirits; and we believe that there is a spiritual desire in the heart as well, with which we were created, which naturally and properly likes God and neighbour, which is in harmony (in consonance, in accordance) with the desire of the Holy Angels. To love God and neighbour in God, we need to be cleansed of the bestial desire. The cleansing is performed by the Holy Spirit in a person who, with his life, is expressing a desire for the cleansing. Actually, the thing that is called the heart, in a moral sense, is the desire and other forces of the soul, but not the body part – the heart. The forces are concentrated in this part – and the common use of the name is transferred from the part to the congregation of forces.

In contrast to the sense of the carnal men, the spiritual men who smelled the fragrance of evil, which pretends to be good, immediately feel an aversion to the books, smelling with this fragrance. A passage from the "Imitation" was read for the elder Isaiah, a monk who was living in stillness in the Nikiforov Pustyn monastery (Olonetsk or Petrozavodsk diocese) and succeeded in noetic prayer and who was granted an overshadowing of grace. The elder immediately went deeply into the meaning of the book. He laughed and said, "*Oh, this is written from conceit. There is nothing true here! Everything – is invented! What Thomas imagined about the spiritual states and how he fancied about them without knowing them from the experience, the same way he described them.*" Prelest, as a misfortune, represents itself a sad spectacle; as the absurdity, it is – a funny sight. Archimandrite of the Cyril Novoezersk monastery (Novgorod diocese), known for his austere life, and who, in simplicity of the heart, was engaged almost exclusively in the bodily feat and who had a very moderate notion about the feat of the soul, first proposed to the persons who were asking his advices and who were guided by him, to read the book "Imitation"; a few years before his death he began to prohibit reading it, speaking with the holy simplicity: "*Before I acknowledged this book as edifying; but God has revealed me that it is harmful for the soul*". Hieroschemamonk Leonid, known for the active monastic experience, who started the spiritual accomplishment in the Optina Pustyn (Kaluga diocese) had the same opinion about the "Imitation". All of these ascetics were familiar to me personally. – Some landowner, brought up in the spirit of Orthodoxy, who knew well the so-called high society i.e. the world, in the higher echelons of it, once saw the book "Imitation" in the hands of his daughter. He forbade her to read the book, saying: "I do not want you to follow the fashion and flirt with God." That is the most correct evaluation of the book.

Disciple: Are there any other kinds of prelest?

Elder: All particular kinds of self-delusion and delusion by demons belong to the two main types of the above, and occur either from the wrong action of the mind, or wrong action of the heart. The action of "conceit" is especially extensive. Not without reason, the state of mind of those monks who, having rejected the exercise of the Jesus Prayer and generally noetic doing, are satisfied only with one external praying, is attributed to the state of self-delusion and prelest. That is, they attend all the church services and execute their prayer rule, consisting solely of psalms and oral and verbal prayers. They can not avoid "conceit", as the mentioned elder Basil explains this in the preface to the book of the St. Gregory of Sinai, referring mainly to the writings of the saints, this Gregory and St. Symeon the New Theologian. A sign of a crept in "conceit" is revealed in an ascetic in this way: when they think about themselves that they spend an attentive life, they often despise others because of pride, say badly about them, consider themselves worthy, in their conceited opinion, to be the shepherds of the sheep and their leaders, becoming like the blind man pointing the way to other blind men (On the second way of attention and prayer.) Oral and verbal prayer is fruitful when it is associated with attention, which happens very rarely: because we learn the attention mainly during the exercise of the Jesus Prayer